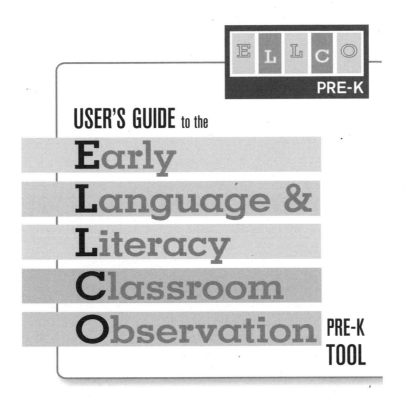

E L L C O
PRE-K

USER'S GUIDE to the

Early Language & Literacy Classroom Observation

PRE-K TOOL

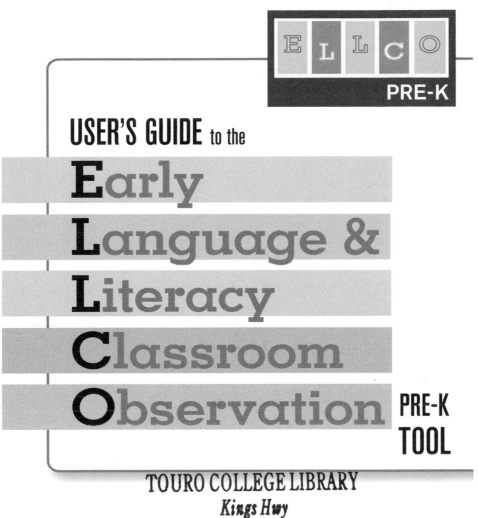

ELLCO PRE-K

USER'S GUIDE to the

Early Language & Literacy Classroom Observation

PRE-K TOOL

by

Miriam W. Smith, Ed.D.
Joanne P. Brady, M.Ed.
& Louisa Anastasopoulos, M.P.P.

Education Development Center, Inc.
Newton, Massachusetts

·P A U L·H·
BROOKES
PUBLISHING C⁰.®

Baltimore • London • Sydney

KH

·P A U L·H·
BROOKES
PUBLISHING C⁰ ®

is a registered trademark owned by
Paul H. Brookes Publishing Co., Inc.

To contact the publisher: Paul H. Brookes Publishing Co.,
Post Office Box 10624, Baltimore, Maryland 21285-0624
1-800-638-3775; 1-410-337-9580; fax: 1-410-337-8539
www.brookespublishing.com

The *Early Childhood Language and Literacy Classroom Observation Tool, Pre-K
(ELLCO Pre-K),* is intended for one-time use only and can be purchased in packages
of five (under ISBN-13: 978-1-55766-947-6). To order, contact Brookes Publishing Co.

For information on bulk sales, contact Brookes Publishing's Sales Manager at
sales@brookespublishing.com, or call Brookes at one of the numbers listed above.

For information on arranging training for the ELLCO Pre-K, please contact Brookes
Publishing Co.

The case studies in this book are based on the authors' experience. Names and identifying
details have been changed to protect privacy.

Typeset by Integrated Publishing Solutions, Grand Rapids, Michigan.
Manufactured in the United States of America by
Sheridan Books, Inc., Chelsea, Michigan.

Library of Congress Cataloging-in-Publication Data

Smith, Miriam W.
   User's guide to the early language and literacy classroom observation tool, pre-K
(Ellco pre-K) / by Miriam W. Smith, Joanne P. Brady & Louisa Anastasopoulos.
      p.   cm.
   Rev. ed. of: User's guide to the early language & literacy classroom observation toolkit.
   Includes bibliographical references.
   ISBN-13: 978-1-55766-946-9 (pbk.)
   ISBN-10: 1-55766-946-5 (pbk.)
   1. English language—Study and teaching (Primary)   2. English language—Study and teaching
(Preschool)   3. Language arts (Early childhood)   4. Language acquisition.   I. Brady, Joanne P.
II. Anastasopoulos, Louisa.   III. Smith, Miriam W. User's guide to the early language & literacy
classroom observation toolkit.   IV. Title.
LB1528.S575 2008
372.6—dc22

2007037168

British Library Cataloguing in Publication data are available from the British Library.

2012   2011   2010   2009   2008

10   9   8   7   6   5   4   3   2   1

8/17/11

Contents

About the Authors

Miriam W. Smith, Ed.D., Consultant, Education Development Center, Inc. (EDC), 55 Chapel Street, Newton, Massachusetts 02458

Dr. Smith has always enjoyed working directly with young children and teachers of young children. Beginning in 1987, she collected and analyzed data for the longitudinal Home–School Study of Language and Literacy Development. Her work on that project brought her into many classrooms as an observer and researcher and propelled her interest in classroom environments and practices that promote children's early language and literacy development. Later work conducted for the Center for Children & Families at EDC cemented her commitment to working directly with teachers, supervisors, and education leaders to promote conditions that positively affect children's learning. Currently a consultant to EDC, Dr. Smith continues to engage in research, writing, and professional development with teachers of young children. An active volunteer in local schools and child care programs, she most enjoys spending time in the "living lab" of daily life with her three children.

Joanne P. Brady, M.Ed., Vice President and Director, Center for Children & Families, Education Development Center, Inc., 55 Chapel Street, Newton, Massachusetts 02458

Ms. Brady is recognized nationwide for her contributions to the field of early childhood education. She provides leadership to a range of complex projects that focus on research, assessment, technical assistance, and professional development that translates research and recommended practice into useful programs and products for practitioners and policy makers. Her groundbreaking work with the National Board for Professional Teaching Standards has led to a performance-based assessment to certify accomplished early childhood teachers. In recent years, Ms. Brady has concentrated her efforts on the design of professional development approaches that build teachers' knowledge and skill in content areas, especially language and literacy. Ms. Brady and her colleagues are examining the impact of literacy-related professional development on teachers' practices and children's learning. Ms. Brady presents her work at major conferences and seminars in the United States and abroad and has contributed to numerous publications, including *Critical Issues in Early Childhood Professional Development* (Zaslow & Martinez-Beck, Paul H. Brookes Publishing Co., 2006).

Louisa Anastasopoulos, M.P.P., Project Director, Education Development Center, Inc. (EDC), 55 Chapel Street, Newton, Massachusetts 02458

Ms. Anastasopoulos has extensive knowledge of early language and literacy development and a decade of experience managing language- and literacy-related research projects at the Center for Children & Families at EDC. In addition to her research experience, Ms. Anastasopoulos has codeveloped and serves as the lead instructor of an ELLCO training-of-trainers seminar that prepares teams of qualified professionals to provide ELLCO training. Ms. Anastasopoulos earned a master's degree in public policy with a focus on education from the Georgetown Public Policy Institute.

Acknowledgments

The Early Language and Literacy Classroom Observation Tool, Pre-K, is built on a body of work undertaken at the Center for Children & Families at Education Development Center, Inc. (EDC), from 1997 onward. When the initial ELLCO Toolkit was published in 2002, it represented substantial contributions from many staff. In particular, the current authors want to thank David K. Dickinson, who was instrumental in the development of the initial ELLCO, for his efforts and many contributions.

Over the intervening years, many early childhood practitioners and researchers have used the ELLCO across the country. Their feedback and suggestions have helped to guide this revision. Specifically, we appreciate the thoughtful comments and careful reviews provided by Nancy Clark-Chiarelli, Julie Hirschler, Christina Silvi, and Sue Washburn. We also thank Jean Foley and Lucas Butler for their support in producing the manuscript and their unflagging attention to detail. Finally, we appreciate the editorial support and encouragement received from the Paul H. Brookes Publishing Co. team throughout the revision process. Many thanks to Heather Shrestha, Editorial Director; Astrid Zuckerman, Acquisitions Editor; and Mika Smith, Editorial Supervisor.

Finally, we wish to thank the many early childhood program directors, teachers, and literacy coaches who welcomed us into their programs and classrooms. They have been critical partners in the process, willing to share a slice of classroom life with our team.

Introduction

Since the mid-1980s, it has become increasingly apparent that literacy development begins well before children enter kindergarten. A growing body of research demonstrates the positive role that high-quality early childhood classrooms can play in nourishing children's language and literacy skills (Peisner-Feinberg et al., 1999; Whitehurst et al., 1994) and preventing later reading difficulties (Ramey & Ramey, 2003; Snow, Burns, & Griffin, 1998). Although many researchers agree that some programs are doing a good job in many ways, there is widespread recognition that programs could be made even better—especially by improving practice in key early learning areas such as literacy (Barnett, 2002; U.S. Department of Health and Human Services, Administration for Children and Families, Administration on Children, Youth and Families, Head Start Bureau, 2003; U.S. Department of Health and Human Services, Administration for Children and Families, Project Team FACES, 2003). In an era when early learning standards are being set in place, the Early Language and Literacy Classroom Observation Tool, Pre-K (ELLCO Pre-K), provides an effective way for practitioners, researchers, and others concerned with quality improvement to gauge progress and focus their program improvement efforts.

The ELLCO was first published in 2002 as the ELLCO Toolkit, Research Edition, and has been revised to incorporate the most recent research on early language and literacy development. Now part of a suite of products, the ELLCO Pre-K is an observation instrument that has been expressly designed for use in center-based classrooms for 3- to 5-year-old children. An additional observation instrument completes the set: The ELLCO K–3, Research Edition, is available for use in kindergarten through third grade. A similar tool that was derived from the ELLCO, the Child and Home Early Language and Literacy Observation (CHELLO; Neuman, Dwyer, & Koh, 2007) has been developed for use in family child care and other home-based settings. Together, these items provide practitioners and researchers with tools that describe the extent to which children at different stages of development are receiving optimal support in specific settings for their language and literacy development.

ORGANIZATION OF THE ELLCO PRE-K

The ELLCO Pre-K consists of an observation instrument and a teacher interview designed to supplement the observation. The observation contains a total of 19 items, organized into five main sections.

- Section I: Classroom Structure contains four items that address classroom organization and contents, children's access to and use of materials, management practices, and adult roles and professional focus.

- Section II: Curriculum consists of three items that address the curriculum environment, instructional strategies, opportunities for child choice and initiative, and responsiveness to and reflection of diversity.

- Section III: The Language Environment includes four items that focus on the discourse climate in the classroom, opportunities for extended conversations, vocabulary development, and efforts to develop phonological awareness.

- Section IV: Books and Book Reading contains five items that address the organization and use of the book area, the characteristics of books available, the presence and use of books across content areas of the curriculum, and the quality and frequency of book reading.

- Section V: Print and Early Writing includes three items that focus on the availability of writing materials, opportunities that build awareness of print and varied purposes of writing, instructional strategies, and use of environmental print.

The ELLCO Pre-K is scored and tabulated so that there are two main subscales. Sections I and II combine to create the *General Classroom Environment* subscale. Sections III, IV, and V join together to create the *Language and Literacy* subscale. These subscales are intentionally differentiated, with the emphasis placed on the *Language and Literacy* subscale, which contains the majority of items (12), whereas the *General Classroom Environment* subscale includes the remaining items (7).

UNDERLYING ASSUMPTIONS OF THE ELLCO PRE-K

The ELLCO Pre-K is based on several central assumptions about the nature of children's early literacy development and the conditions and opportunities in classrooms that either support or detract from such development. These central premises follow.

- Opportunities to use and practice oral language and emergent literacy skills are fostered in classrooms that are structured to support children's initiative, actively engage children in learning experiences, and blend goals for other content areas with literacy learning goals.

- Teachers are responsible for encouraging and capitalizing on young children's emergent interest in language and print.

- Teachers are responsible for engaging children in learning activities that teach and reinforce appropriate skills.

- Teachers have a responsibility to understand, evaluate, and respond appropriately to the different literacy skills and learning needs of individuals.

- Connections are made among children's oral language use, the opportunities children have to engage in extended talk, and their emerging early literacy skills.

- Decisions about classroom organization, provision of materials, and scheduling of time are made thoughtfully, with the intent of fostering language, literacy, and learning.

- Teachers plan curricula that support children's language, writing, and reading development and infuse their classrooms with literacy and language.

- Teachers use a range of ongoing assessment techniques to evaluate learning, adjust instruction, communicate with specialists, and coordinate resources and staff efforts.

WHO SHOULD USE THE ELLCO PRE-K?

The developers of ELLCO Pre-K recommend that potential users have strong background knowledge of children's language and literacy development as well as experience teaching in preschool classrooms. The previous version (the

ELLCO Toolkit, Research Edition) has been used by a range of professionals across the country for a variety of purposes, including the following:

- Researchers who are engaged in evaluating the quality of language and literacy practices in early childhood classrooms

- Supervisors and coaches/mentors, trained in early literacy, who are involved in supporting the development of preschool teachers

- Professional development facilitators who are interested in fostering a shared vision of effective early literacy instruction and who want to use a tool that can provide both a springboard for discussion and a means for systematic documentation of progress

- Teachers who are interested in a reflective tool for assessing their classroom practices and strategies

HOW DOES THE ELLCO PRE-K COMPARE WITH THE ELLCO TOOLKIT?

Thanks to the widespread use of the original ELLCO Toolkit, Research Edition, and feedback from a diverse body of users, we have incorporated a range of changes. These changes serve to make the ELLCO Pre-K more focused than the original ELLCO, as well as easier to use and score. Items from the Literacy Environment Checklist[1] and Literacy Activities Rating Scale have been integrated into the architecture of the observation itself. The purpose of this substantial change was to make several of the observation items more robust by including the details previously gathered by the Literacy Environment Checklist and the Literacy Activities Rating Scale and to reduce some of the previous reliance on counting literacy materials and activities that tended to skew results toward classrooms that had more "stuff," regardless of whether or how that stuff was used. The ELLCO Pre-K explicitly values *how* materials are used by teachers and children more than whether materials are merely present in the classroom. We have also increased the specificity and range of important early literacy skills that are observed, such as phonological awareness, efforts to increase spoken vocabulary, and uses of environmental print. The most significant and requested change is the inclusion of detailed descriptive indicators for each of the five scale points (rather than just for three of the scale points), which will help observers more clearly and reliably decide how to score each item.

---

[1]The Literacy Environment Checklist will continue to be made available by Brookes Publishing. See http://www.brookespublishing.com/ellco for details on obtaining the Literacy Environment Checklist. This will enable grantees to supply the U.S. Department of Education with the necessary data required by the Government Performance and Results Act of 1993 (PL 103-62).

CONTENTS OF THE USER'S GUIDE

The remaining six chapters of this user's guide provide detailed support to enable practitioners and researchers to understand how to score the ELLCO Pre-K and use it for different purposes.

- Chapter 2, "Effective Elements of Early Literacy: Kendra's Story," uses a series of vignettes of a preschool child's experiences in the classroom to illustrate key components of early literacy. It also demonstrates the way that everyday events can be translated into evidence to support ratings of ELLCO Pre-K items.

- Chapter 3, "Structure of the ELLCO Pre-K," addresses the content of each section, the architecture of items, and the contents of the Teacher Interview.

- Chapter 4, "How to Conduct an ELLCO Observation," offers specific guidelines for scheduling and preparing for a classroom visit, general strategies for rating items, and ways to avoid bias in scoring items.

- Chapter 5, "A Review of Sample Items," walks the user through the steps in rating three different items. Classroom vignettes, sample evidence, and explanatory text simulate how an observer translates what was seen and heard into a score for specific items.

- Chapter 6, "Using the ELLCO Pre-K for Professional Development," discusses how the instrument itself and various components of the user's guide can be used as an effective vehicle for promoting teacher reflection and collective responsibility for children's learning. It offers guidelines for building the ELLCO Pre-K into an ongoing professional development initiative and provides practical ideas that are tied to each of the five sections of the tool.

- Chapter 7, "Using the ELLCO Pre-K in Research," describes the characteristics of effective data collector training, including criteria for selecting observers, approaches to achieving and calculating interrater reliability, and recalibrating observers in the field.

A technical appendix principally describes the psychometric properties of the ELLCO Toolkit, Research Edition, in preschool classrooms, including information on interrater reliability, internal validity, test–retest reliability, correlations among the tools, and correlations with other early childhood observation instruments. A matrix also is provided in the technical appendix (Table A.15) that illustrates the comparability of the constructs measured in the ELLCO Toolkit, Research Edition, and the ELLCO Pre-K. The resources list at the end of the book is devoted to a variety of resources, including an annotated set of web sites, web-based resources, articles, and books that are relevant to early literacy research and practice.

REFERENCES

Barnett, W.S. (2002). *The battle over Head Start: What the research shows.* Retrieved August 5, 2003, from http://nieer.org/resources/research/BattleHeadStart.pdf

Neuman, S.B., Dwyer, J., & Koh, S. (2007). *Child/Home Early Language and Literacy Observation (CHELLO) Tool.* Baltimore: Paul H. Brookes Publishing Co.

Peisner-Feinberg, E.S., Burchinal, M.R., Clifford, R.M., Yazejian, N., Culkin, M.L., Zelazo, J., et al. (1999). *The children of the Cost, Quality, and Outcomes Study go to school* (Tech. Rep.). Chapel Hill: University of North Carolina at Chapel Hill, FPG Child Development Institute.

Ramey, C.T., & Ramey, S.L. (2003, February). *Preparing America's children for success in school.* Paper presented at the annual meeting of the National Governors Association, Washington, DC.

Snow, C.E., Burns, M.S., & Griffin, P. (Eds.). (1998). *Preventing reading difficulties in young children.* Washington, DC: National Academies Press.

U.S. Department of Health and Human Services, Administration for Children and Families, Administration on Children, Youth and Families, Head Start Bureau. (2003). *Strengthening Head Start: What the evidence shows.* Washington, DC: Author.

U.S. Department of Health and Human Services, Administration for Children and Families, Project Team FACES. (2003). *Head Start FACES 2000: A whole-child perspective on program performance. Fourth progress report.* Washington, DC: U.S. Department of Health and Human Services, Administration for Children and Families, Administration on Children, Youth and Families, Child Outcomes Research and Evaluation, Head Start Bureau.

Whitehurst, G.J., Epstein, J.N., Angell, A.C., Payne, A.C., Crone, D.A., & Fischel, J.E. (1994). Outcomes of an emergent literacy intervention in Head Start. *Journal of Educational Psychology, 86,* 542–555.

Effective Elements of Early Literacy

Kendra's Story

Using the ELLCO Pre-K gives educators and researchers a concrete way to examine the literacy-related features of classrooms. One of the goals of the ELLCO Pre-K and its user's guide is to help early childhood educators improve the quality of the literacy and language learning taking place in their classrooms by providing a better understanding of which practices promote such learning. Kendra's Story can help teachers and observers grasp the context for and importance of observing and rating literacy-related practices and materials in a classroom. Kendra's Story also can function as a starting point from which teachers brainstorm ways to improve their own practices and foster children's early experiences with language and print. It can be used either after the ELLCO Pre-K has been completed or while teachers engage in professional development.

The vignettes that follow and the corresponding ELLCO Pre-K items are not intended to be an exhaustive picture of an ELLCO Pre-K observation. Instead, they are illustrative of the types of activities and exchanges one might see when visiting a classroom of 3- and 4-year-olds. These vignettes, extracted from Kendra's day, offer a picture of where evidence for rating ELLCO Pre-K items may be observed within the regular course of classroom events.

Vignette 1: Entering

"Good morning, Kendra, did you want to sign up to go outside?" sang out Miss Denise as Kendra entered her preschool classroom. Miss Denise held out a clipboard and pen for Kendra to use. "Nope. I'm going to color with Lianna," replied Kendra as she hung up her jacket in her cubby and placed her lunchbox with others on a labeled shelf. She added her name to the daily sign-in sheet on a low table next to the cubbies, then headed off to the writing table.

Kendra is a preschool child in a large, urban child care center entering her classroom on a typical day. One of her teachers is on hand to greet her and offers her a choice of activity to sign up for on a clipboard. Kendra declines that option, stating her preference to join a peer at another activity. It is clear that Kendra's classroom and teachers have empowered her to be independent in her activities and allowed her to make choices based on her own interests and peer affiliation. Providing regular opportunities for children to make choices of activities helps support their development as active, engaged learners (Bowman, Donovan, & Burns, 2001; Strickland & Snow, 2002).

This vignette also shows Kendra's familiarity with several organizational and literacy routines of her classroom: She independently stores her belongings in her own labeled cubby, knows where to place her lunchbox, and knows that the schedule for this point in the day allows her to choose which learning center she wants to work in. She also participates in a daily literacy routine as she independently signs in for the day. A classroom environment that is intentionally structured to support children's independence fosters children's sense of belonging and their ability to affect their own learning community (Farran, Aydogan, Kang, & Lipsey, 2006; Justice, 2004; Roskos & Neuman, 2001). In addition, participation in regular, systematic literacy routines, such as reading labels and signing names, provides children with beginning knowledge of the functions of print and supports their own initial efforts to create meaningful print (Whitehurst et al., 1994). In an actual ELLCO Pre-K observation, evidence from this vignette might support ratings for the following items:

Item 1, Organization of the Classroom

Item 6, Opportunities for Child Choice and Initiative

Item 18, Support for Children's Writing

Vignette 2: At the Writing Table

Kendra identified a small chair at the table next to her friend, sat down, and surveyed the materials around her. She found paper of various sizes and shapes, chunky crayons, markers, a few small pairs of scissors, and two tape dispensers. "Whoa! What are these?" Kendra exclaimed, picking up some clear plastic alphabet stencils. Miss Rosa, seated at the sand table nearby, explained that they were stencils that could be used to write things. Kendra selected a piece of yellow paper and a chunky red crayon, carefully placed the stencil on the paper (backward) and attempted to trace the letter *K*. "Miss Rosa! This doesn't work!" said Kendra. Miss Rosa came over and squatted next to Kendra. "Hmm . . . you're right, that looks kind of frustrating. That crayon is sort of big for that stencil. Any ideas about what you could do to make it work better?" Kendra thought for a moment, looked around, then pulled a container of thin colored pencils off a shelf and plunked it onto the table. She selected a green pencil and tried again with the stencils; this time she copied the letters *K, L,* and *E,* then stopped. She wrote her name in red marker at the top of her paper. "There," said Kendra, satisfied with her results (see Figure 2.1). She scooped up her paper and took it over to a small file box, located the folder marked with her name, and placed her paper inside.

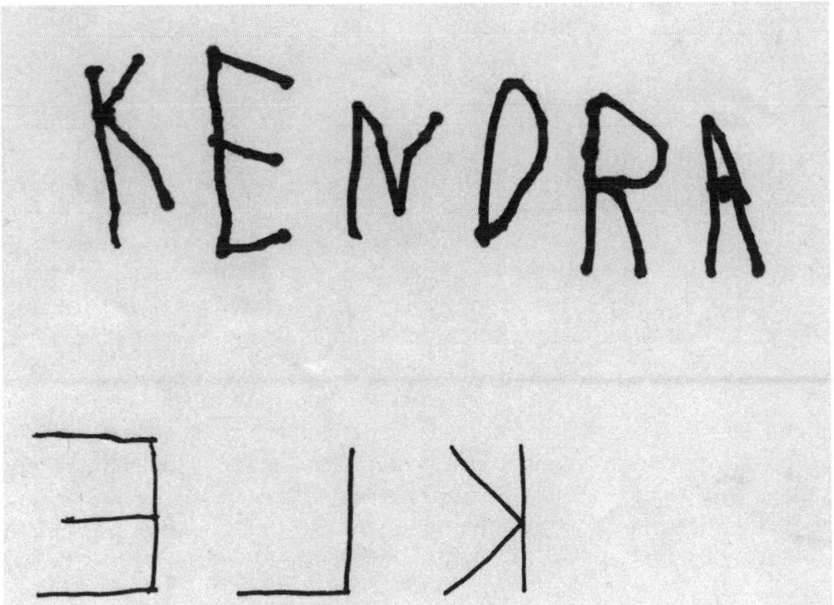

Figure 2.1.   Kendra's handwriting.

In this vignette, we see Kendra getting to work in her chosen activity setting. There is clearly a range of art and writing materials available and accessible, most of which are familiar. Kendra notices some new letter stencils and, with a bit of teacher support, uses them appropriately. When children are offered regular access to writing materials, they are able to explore the functions and forms of writing and with teacher support may begin to write letters, names, words, and short phrases (Schickedanz & Casbergue, 2004). In this vignette, it is notable that the teacher is nearby to offer support, yet she encourages Kendra to try to solve the problem on her own. Teacher support that is flexible and focused on the needs and interests of children supports their learning (Strickland & Snow, 2002). Once again, Kendra shows her knowledge of classroom routines as she independently takes her finished work and stores it in her own file. In an actual ELLCO Pre-K observation, evidence from this vignette might support ratings for the following items:

Item 2, Contents of the Classroom

Item 3, Classroom Management

Item 4, Personnel

Item 8, Discourse Climate

Item 17, Early Writing Environment

Vignette 3: Construction Zone

Kendra and Lianna headed off together to an area of the classroom with a sign reading *Construction Zone* decorated with pictures of houses and buildings in various stages of construction. In addition to blocks of all sizes, there were a variety of cardboard boxes, some tubes and pipes, and many small animal figures. There were baskets on nearby shelves with pinecones, shells, rocks, and sticks. In an adjacent activity center there was fabric, glue, yarn, cotton balls, and sewing supplies. On top of the shelves separating the two areas were clipboards with plain and lined paper and pencils attached to them with string. There were also several books in a basket, including *Castle*, by David Macaulay; *The Busy Building Book*, by Sue Tarsky; *Salamander Room*, by Anne Mazer; and *The Inside-Outside Book of New York City*, by Roxie Munro. On a bulletin board above the construction area was a list of words, written by Miss Denise, entitled *Animal Homes*, which included the following terms:

house	shell
home	nutshell
shelter	barn
tree	kennel
hole	cave
nest	

Kendra and Lianna cleared a space and gathered several small, feathery creatures from the selection of animals. "Let's make a nest!" suggested Lianna. "Okay," replied Kendra. The girls gathered some sticks, fabric, and cotton balls from the sewing center nearby and worked together to build a nest. They then tucked their tiny, feathered figures into their creation. Lianna grabbed a clipboard off the shelf and wrote *S O R*, then scribbled part of it out and rewrote *S T O P* and placed the sign on their nest (see Figure 2.2). The girls called Miss Rosa over to see their creation, and she helped them by writing, *This is our nest. Please be careful.*

In this vignette, Kendra and Lianna are seen engaging in play that builds on their existing knowledge of animal homes and extends their learning as they actively use terms from the word wall and create their own useful environmental print. It is essential to help children learn about the functions of writing by creating print with and for them, relating writing to ongoing curriculum, and displaying print so that it can be used actively (Adams, 1990; Farran et al.,

Figure 2.2.   Lianna's sign for the nest that she and Kendra built, with additional information written by their teacher.

2006). Vocabulary development during the preschool years is critical to children's later development of language and literacy skills; therefore, the inclusion of meaningful vocabulary words within the context of ongoing curriculum is an effective technique that supports children's language learning and vocabulary development (Biemiller, 2006; Dickinson, Cote, & Smith, 1993; Dickinson & Smith, 1994; Snow, Burns, & Griffin, 1998). We also notice that the Construction Zone is organized and outfitted with a wide variety of open-ended materials that could be used for many purposes, and children are free to use them in their own ways. Ample time for play with open-ended materials has been consistently related to positive child learning outcomes during and beyond the preschool years (Pellegrini & Galda, 1993). We also note the inclusion of books in this interest area that appear to be related to a theme of building and homes. Exposure to varied literature and access to literature as reference material are important components of early literacy and are essential building blocks for later literacy as well (Morrow & Gambrell, 2001). Children who are read to frequently, and who participate in choosing and using books during play, develop understanding of book concepts and book language that helps to foster a lifelong interest in books and reading (DeTemple, 2001; Sulzby, 1994). In an actual ELLCO Pre-K observation, evidence from this vignette might support ratings for the following items:

Item 2, Contents of the Classroom

Item 5, Approaches to Curriculum

Item 10, Efforts to Build Vocabulary

Item 13, Characteristics of Books

Item 14, Books for Learning

Item 19, Environmental Print

Vignette 4: Circle Time

Later, during circle time, Miss Denise held up the book *A House Is a House for Me*, by MaryAnn Hoberman. Several children commented that they remembered the book. Miss Denise was seated by a large piece of newsprint on an easel. "Today," she suggested, "let's pick out some new words for places where people or machines might live." As she read the book, some children chanted along, and from time to time Miss Denise stopped to list words on the newsprint, including the following:

castle	hangar
dwelling	dock
tepee	slip
pueblo	terminal
wigwam	earth
garage	

During the reading, there was brief discussion of individual words such as *hangar* that seemed to confuse some of the children. Miss Denise explained that the kind of *hanger* that clothes hang on is a different word. This *hangar* is a shelter for airplanes. She also directed their attention to the picture of an airplane hangar that accompanied the text. At the end of the reading, Miss Denise asked the children to help her reread their list of words and encouraged them to think about which type of shelter they might like to dwell in. At the conclusion of circle time, Miss Denise took the new list of words and hung them next to the list already hung in the Construction Zone.

In this vignette, Kendra and her classmates are engaged in a full-group book reading session. The book is already familiar to the children, and the teacher has prepared in advance for rereading it with the group, choosing to focus on a subset of vocabulary words that tie in with the current curriculum theme. Teaching vocabulary in the context of book reading is a powerful way to help children connect written words with spoken vocabulary (Justice & Kaderavek, 2002; McKeown & Beck, 2006). Discussing word definitions in the context of reading models ways to develop meaning from texts (e.g., comments such as "What do you think it means?" or "What does the picture show?") and may reinforce children's later efforts in reading comprehension (Biemiller, 2006; Neuman, Snow, & Canizares, 2000). A focus on vocabulary words that connect with the curriculum and are reinforced in displays and used throughout the classroom provides additional support for children's word learning and vocabulary use (Farran et al., 2006; Justice, 2004). In an actual ELLCO Pre-K observation, evidence from this vignette might support ratings for the following items:

Item 9, Opportunities for Extended Conversations

Item 10, Efforts to Build Vocabulary

Item 15, Approaches to Book Reading

Item 16, Quality of Book Reading

Vignette 5: Lunch Time

At lunchtime, Kendra sat at a small table with three friends. In a moment of silliness, Shawn put his sandwich on his head. Miss Rosa saw him and reminded him, "Food is for eating, Shawn. Bread does not go on your head!" Ellis noticed that Miss Rosa had rhymed and began chanting "bread head bread head" in a loud voice. Miss Rosa came to the table and sat down with her own lunch. She commented about the rhyming and redirected the children by suggesting a game to find "other words that sound like bread." The children took turns coming up with words, including *bed*, *head*, *dead*, *led*, *Ned*, *shed*, *qued*, and *med*. There was much hilarity, especially for the nonsense words.

In this vignette, the children are enjoying a spirited lunchtime. When their silliness begins to get out of control, the teacher reins it in by engaging them in a word-play activity. Her manner is firm but playful, respectful of children's interests while gently guiding their participation. She seizes an opportunity to build on their budding awareness of sounds in language and subtly supports their language and literacy learning. Rhyming is a key component of phonological awareness and an important precursor to phonemic awareness (Adams, 1990; Bryant, MacLean, Bradley, & Crossland, 1990; Scarborough, 1998). In an actual ELLCO Pre-K observation, evidence from this vignette might support ratings for the following items:

Item 3, Classroom Management

Item 8, Discourse Climate

Item 11, Phonological Awareness

Vignette 6: Ready to Go Home

Near the end of her school day, Kendra returned to the coloring table. This time, she took out a piece of white paper and a marker. She carefully drew a house, then added two letters in front of it (see Figure 2.3).

In this final vignette, we see Kendra returning to the writing area, the place where she began her day. Clearly, the current classroom theme is relevant and motivating to Kendra. She draws a house, complete with windows, doors, and roof, then labels it *M Y*—my house! Once again we see evidence of a child's engagement in classroom curriculum and natural connections made to emergent literacy. In an actual ELLCO Pre-K observation, evidence from this vignette might support ratings for the following items:

Item 5, Approaches to Curriculum (pursuing theme independently)

Item 17, Early Writing Environment

These vignettes have demonstrated emergent literacy in action in a typical preschool classroom. As children played and interacted with each other and with their teacher, they engaged in a wide range of behaviors, many of which reflected their growing understanding of the functions and nature of reading and writing. They understood that signs could convey important messages, that spoken words can be written down and read, and that words are made up of sounds that correspond to written symbols. *Emergent literacy* is the phase of literacy development during which young children come to understand the many features and functions of the spoken and printed word. During this period they do not read and write in conventional ways, but through their attempts at reading and writing their language, they reveal their emerging understandings of literacy.

Figure 2.3.   Kendra's house.

REFERENCES

Adams, M.J. (1990). *Beginning to read: Thinking and learning about print.* Cambridge, MA: MIT Press.

Biemiller, A. (2006). Vocabulary development and instruction: A prerequisite for school learning. In D.K. Dickinson & S.B. Neuman (Eds.), *Handbook of early literacy research* (Vol. 2, pp. 41–51). New York: Guilford Press.

Bowman, B., Donovan, M.S., & Burns, M.S. (2001). *Eager to learn: Educating our preschoolers.* Washington, DC: National Academies Press.

Bryant, P.E., MacLean, M., Bradley, L.L., & Crossland, J. (1990). Rhyme and alliteration, phoneme detection, and learning to read. *Developmental Psychology, 26,* 429–438.

DeTemple, J.M. (2001). Parents and children reading books together. In D.K. Dickinson & P.O. Tabors (Eds.), *Beginning literacy with language: Young children learning at home and school* (pp. 31–51). Baltimore: Paul H. Brookes Publishing Co.

Dickinson, D.K., Cote, L., & Smith, M.W. (1993). Learning vocabulary in preschool: Social and discourse contexts affecting vocabulary growth. In C. Daiute (Ed.), *The development of literacy through social interaction* (pp. 67–78). San Francisco: Jossey-Bass.

Dickinson, D.K., & Smith, M.W. (1994). Long-term effects of preschool teachers' book readings on low-income children's vocabulary and story comprehension. *Reading Research Quarterly, 29*(2), 104–122.

Farran, D.C., Aydogan, C., Kang, S.J., & Lipsey, M.W. (2006). Preschool classroom environments and the quantity and quality of children's literacy and language behaviors. In D.K. Dickinson & S.B. Neuman (Eds.), *Handbook of early literacy research* (Vol. 2, pp. 257–268). New York: Guilford Press.

Justice, L.M. (2004). Creating language-rich preschool classroom environments. *Teaching Exceptional Children, 37*(2), 36–44.

Justice, L.M., & Kaderavek, J. (2002). Using shared storybook reading to promote emergent literacy. *Teaching Exceptional Children, 34*(4), 8–13.

McKeown, M.G., & Beck, I.L. (2006). Encouraging young children's language interactions with stories. In D.K. Dickinson & S.B. Neuman (Eds.), *Handbook of early literacy research* (Vol. 2, pp. 281–294). New York: Guilford Press.

Morrow, L.M., & Gambrell, L.B. (2001). Literature-based instruction in the early years. In S.B. Neuman & D.K. Dickinson (Eds.), *Handbook of early literacy research* (pp. 348–360). New York: Guilford Press.

Neuman, S., Snow, C.E., & Canizares, S. (2000). *Building language for literacy.* New York: Scholastic.

Pellegrini, A.D., & Galda, L. (1993). Ten years after: A reexamination of symbolic play and literacy research. *Reading Research Quarterly, 28*(2), 163–175.

Roskos, K., & Neuman, S.B. (2001). Environment and its influences for early literacy teaching and learning. In S.B. Neuman & D.K. Dickinson (Eds.), *Handbook of early literacy research* (pp. 281–292). New York: Guilford Press.

Scarborough, H.S. (1998). Early identification of children at risk for reading disabilities: Phonological awareness and some other promising predictors. In B.K. Shapiro, P.J. Accardo, & A.J. Capute (Eds.), *Specific reading disability: A view of the spectrum.* Timonium, MD: York Press.

Schickedanz, J.A., & Casbergue, R.M. (2004). *Writing in preschool: Learning to orchestrate meaning and marks.* Newark, DE: International Reading Association.

Snow, C.E., Burns, S.M., & Griffin, P. (Eds.). (1998). *Preventing reading difficulties in young children.* Washington, DC: National Academies Press.

Strickland, D., & Snow, C.E. (2002). *Preparing our teachers: Opportunities for better reading instruction.* Washington, DC: Joseph Henry Press.

Sulzby, E. (1994). Children's emergent reading of favorite storybooks: A developmental study. In R.B. Ruddell, M.R. Ruddell, & H. Singer (Eds.), *Theoretical models and processes of reading* (4th ed., pp. 244–280). Newark, DE: International Reading Association.

Whitehurst, G.J., Epstein, J.N., Angell, A.C., Payne, A.C., Crone, D.A., & Fischel, J.E. (1994). Outcomes of an emergent literacy intervention in Head Start. *Journal of Educational Psychology, 86,* 542–555.

3

Structure of
the ELLCO Pre-K

OVERALL STRUCTURE AND LEVELS

As described in Chapter 1, the ELLCO Pre-K comprises 19 items, grouped into five main sections (see Table 3.1). Each item is designed to capture important and observable aspects of language and literacy in the preschool classroom. While each item is unique in its focus, all items are uniform with respect to their structure.

Each item is constructed to describe the characteristics of classroom practice at five distinct levels, from *exemplary* to *deficient*, with the highest number indicating the most accomplished level of performance. Therefore, Level 5 indicates *exemplary* practice; Level 4 indicates *strong* practice; Level 3 indicates *basic* practice; Level 2 indicates *inadequate* practice; and Level 1 indicates *deficient* practice.

Each item consists of anchor statements for each level, as well as descriptive indicators, which are provided as scoring guidance for each item. An evidence page is provided for each item, to allow for detailed recording of pertinent evidence observed during the classroom visit. The following sections discuss the anchor statements, descriptive indicators, and evidence pages in further detail.

The ELLCO Pre-K also includes a Teacher Interview, a brief and supplementary component of the classroom observation, and a score form for summarizing and totaling scores. The Teacher Interview is discussed briefly in this chapter. Chapter 4 provides detailed information on conducting an observation and interview and using the score form.

Table 3.1.   Structure of the ELLCO Pre-K

GENERAL CLASSROOM ENVIRONMENT

Section I: Classroom Structure

Item 1: Organization of the Classroom

Item 2: Contents of the Classroom

Item 3: Classroom Management

Item 4: Personnel

Section II: Curriculum

Item 5: Approaches to Curriculum

Item 6: Opportunities for Child Choice and Initiative

Item 7: Recognizing Diversity in the Classroom

LANGUAGE AND LITERACY

Section III: The Language Environment

Item 8: Discourse Climate

Item 9: Opportunities for Extended Conversations

Item 10: Efforts to Build Vocabulary

Item 11: Phonological Awareness

Section IV: Books and Book Reading

Item 12: Organization of Book Area

Item 13: Characteristics of Books

Item 14: Books for Learning

Item 15: Approaches to Book Reading

Item 16: Quality of Book Reading

Section V: Print and Early Writing

Item 17: Early Writing Environment

Item 18: Support for Children's Writing

Item 19: Environmental Print

ANCHOR STATEMENTS

Associated with each level is an anchor statement that has been devised for each item. The intent of this overarching statement is to capture the essence of the practice that is being rated and the nature and quality of evidence required to assign a particular score. Although each item demands different content, anchor statements across all items have a consistent element. At each scale point, the orienting language contains a key word, in boldface, to signal the strength of evidence required to assign that score.

- All *exemplary* items begin with the phrase, "There is **compelling** evidence . . . "

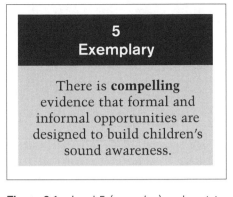

Figure 3.1. Level 5 (*exemplary*) anchor statement for ELLCO Pre-K Item 11, Phonological Awareness.

- All *strong* items begin with the phrase, "There is **sufficient** evidence . . . "

- All *basic* items begin with the phrase, "There is **some** evidence . . . "

- All *inadequate* items begin with the phrase, "There is **limited** evidence . . . "

- All *deficient* items begin with the phrase, "There is **minimal** evidence . . . "

This pairing of rating level and key word is intended to help raters differentiate among levels of practice observed. For example, see Figure 3.1 for the Level 5 (*exemplary*) anchor statement for Item 11, Phonological Awareness. The anchor statement is critical in determining a rating. It alerts the observer to watch and listen for formal and informal activities and interactions that provide opportunities for children to develop phonological awareness skills.

DESCRIPTIVE INDICATORS

The anchor statement at each level is followed by a series of bulleted statements, called *descriptive indicators*, which provide more detail about the types and quality of practice that should be observed in order to assign a particular score. It is essential that observers understand that the descriptive indicators are *not* intended to be a checklist. Instead they are guideposts and exemplars that help to distinguish one level from another. If we examine the first descriptive indicator for Item 11: Phonological Awareness, we can see that Level 5 (*exemplary*) is characterized by the following description:

> *Teachers engage children in varied interactions designed to build their awareness of sounds in language through planned and playful*

activities (e.g., rhyming, segmenting words into syllables, alliteration). Teachers designate time, whether formal or informal (e.g., wait time) to encouraging children to listen for and use the sounds of language apart from their meaning or written form.

In comparison, the descriptive indicator for Level 4 (*strong*) suggests a qualitative difference (emphasis added):

*Teachers engage children in varied interactions designed to build their awareness of sounds in language through planned and playful activities, **though their activities may be somewhat less engaging.** Teachers designate time, whether formal or informal (e.g., wait time) to encouraging children to listen for and use the sounds of language, **but there may be fewer opportunities.***

The Level 4 descriptive indicator clearly demonstrates that teachers are planning and carrying out phonological awareness activities and are setting aside time for children to explore the sounds of language. However, the first descriptive indicator points to two aspects of the practice that may shift, as noted by the boldface, italicized phrases just mentioned. Observers are guided to notice and record the children's level of engagement as they participate in phonological awareness activities as well as the extent of the opportunities available for such explorations with sounds.

As you proceed across the descriptive indicator for rating Item 11 to Level 2 (*inadequate*), observers' content knowledge about phonological awareness forcefully comes into play. Level 2 is characterized as follows (emphasis added):

*While teachers carry out activities that **involve children with the sounds of language** (e.g., nursery rhymes and songs), there is limited evidence that they **are intentionally building children's sound awareness.** They may also create confusion for children by confounding sounds with letter names.*

At this level it is clear that teachers may sing with children and use nursery rhymes as a part of their practice, but they do not appear to call attention to the rhymes or other sound units (e.g., syllables, initial sounds). Furthermore, they may introduce confusion by shifting children's attention away from the sounds to letters or, through their interactions with children, demonstrate a misconception or incomplete understanding of phonological awareness.

Taken together, the anchor statement and descriptive indicators represent the qualitative rubric for rating each item. Although these elements are common across items, the nature of the evidence examined and the contents of rubrics are fashioned specifically for each item. Therefore, observers should be very familiar with the rubric before observing a classroom.

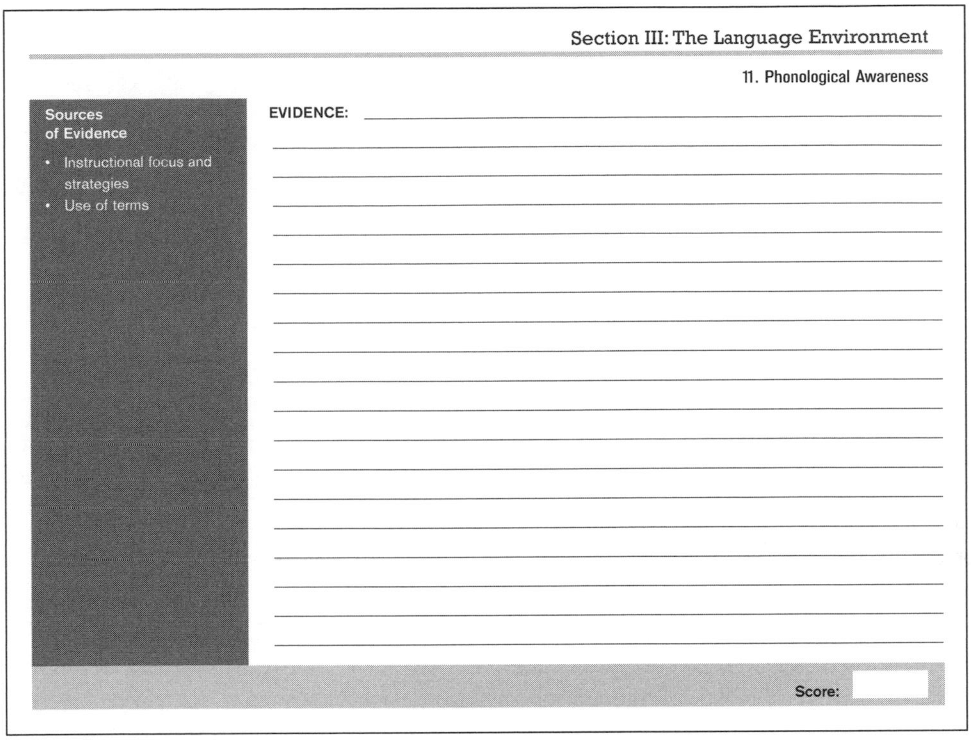

Section III: The Language Environment

11. Phonological Awareness

Sources of Evidence

- Instructional focus and strategies
- Use of terms

EVIDENCE:

Score:

Figure 3.2. Evidence section for ELLCO Pre-K Item 11, Phonological Awareness.

EVIDENCE SECTION

In addition, we have added an evidence section for each item. We have provided summary words and/or phrases to help observers quickly and accurately focus on the type of evidence necessary to score the item. For example, for Item 11, Phonological Awareness, we direct observers to take data on the *instructional focus and strategies* and *use of terms* (see Figure 3.2).

TEACHER INTERVIEW

The ELLCO Pre-K instrument is followed by a set of brief Teacher Interview questions that can be used to gather information to supplement or provide context for observed data. Interview questions are not to be used as evidence in and of themselves but to elucidate specific aspects of the observation and evidence noted.

4

How to Conduct an ELLCO Pre-K Observation

GUIDELINES FOR OBSERVING IN CLASSROOMS

Scheduling and Duration of Observations

Prior to conducting an ELLCO Pre-K observation, contact the classroom teacher to explain the general purpose of your visit. Work with the teacher to choose a day for your visit in hopes of getting as typical a picture of the classroom as possible. For example, do not schedule your visit on a day when special activities or visitors are planned. You should also obtain information about the classroom schedule and time your observation accordingly. Allow at least 3.5 hours for your visit to ensure that you collect ample evidence to score all of the ELLCO Pre-K items. Plan to observe not only free-choice time and full-group book reading but also a variety of other activities, such as a mealtime, greeting or departing, and any other instructional time. It is important to see teachers interacting with children in various settings in order to get an accurate picture of the language environment and the types of conversations that take place between teachers and children and among children.

In addition to selecting the appropriate day and time for your visit, your initial telephone conversation with the teacher can also provide information needed to complete some items on the cover page and Observation Record page. Ask the teacher for information that will enable you to complete background information, such as the program, center, and teacher information; the duration of the classroom day; the age ranges of children and numbers of children with identified disabilities; the number of English language learners; the primary language spoken in the classroom; and languages spoken by English language learners. The remaining items on the Observation Record page should be completed at the time of the observation.

Conducting Observations with Professionalism and Respect

Classroom observations can be an anxiety-provoking experience for teachers. As the observer, you can help teachers feel more comfortable by taking care to treat them respectfully throughout the entire process. Remember that you are a guest in the classroom. Be sure to greet all teaching staff, introduce yourself, and thank them for allowing you to observe. Remind them how long you plan on staying and indicate that you will do your best to keep out of their way.

Although you will need to position yourself in order to see and hear everything that goes on during your observation, make an effort to be as unobtrusive as possible. In order to ensure that you do not influence what you are trying to observe, you should minimize your impact on the classroom. After your initial greeting, do not interact with the children or the adults, and maintain a neutral facial expression regardless of what you might see or hear during the observation. Children may approach you with questions or comments, but a simple explanation that you are there to see what they are learning and are not able to play is usually enough to satisfy their curiosity.

Preparing for the Observation

Before conducting an observation, you should carefully read through all of the ELLCO Pre-K items several times to familiarize yourself with the content and sequence of the items. Be sure that you thoroughly understand what evidence is needed to rate each item before your visit, so that you can focus your attention on the classroom activities during your observation. You may wish to highlight or circle key words and phrases to help you focus on the most important features of each item.

The ELLCO Pre-K is a sophisticated observation tool that requires you to use your judgment as a professional who is knowledgeable about preschools as well as early language and literacy practices. It is, therefore, strongly recommended that observers have a background in early childhood education and prior experience conducting classroom observations. Specific ELLCO Pre-K training also will help ensure that the tool is administered appropriately. For more information about available training, contact Paul H. Brookes Publishing Co.

TAKING EVIDENCE AND RATING ITEMS

Focusing on the Evidence

Rating each ELLCO Pre-K item is based on the evidence you note throughout your observation. What is evidence? Evidence is represented in the notes that describe what you saw and heard in relation to each item. Classrooms are inherently complex places, and recording evidence can be challenging due to the nonlinear nature of classroom life. Observers should be prepared to flip through the tool in order to record evidence in the correct places. To help you focus your observation and note taking, the ELLCO Pre-K provides summary phrases that are helpful reminders. For example, for Item 1, Organization of the Classroom, the evidence you should look for includes furnishings and comfort, arrangement of interest areas, traffic flow, and independent access (see Figure 4.1).

Section I: Classroom Structure

1. Organization of the Classroom

Sources of Evidence

- Furnishings and comfort
- Arrangement of interest areas
- Traffic flow
- Independent access to materials

EVIDENCE: ______________________

Score: ______

Figure 4.1. Evidence page for ELLCO Pre-K Item 1, Organization of the Classroom.

There are several items for which evidence can and should be gathered at a time when children are not present in the classroom, either prior to their arrival or during outdoor play. These items all deal with classroom materials, and it will be both easier and less intrusive to examine them when the classroom is empty. The items are

- Item 2, Contents of the Classroom

- Item 12, Organization of Book Area

- Item 13, Characteristics of Books

- Item 14, Books for Learning

- Item 17, Early Writing Environment

Rating Strategies

There are two main strategies that can help you in assigning ratings for the ELLCO Pre-K items. One tip that will add structure and focus to your scoring decisions is to start by reading the Level 5 anchor statements and descriptive indicators to determine if you can assign the highest possible score. If the evidence does not support a Level 5 rating, then move on to the Level 4 description. Continue to work your way down until you find the level that best matches the evidence you have noted.

A second strategy is useful when the evidence is mixed or uneven. There may be occasions when a classroom exhibits characteristics that fall under more than one level for a particular item. Using Item 2, Contents of the Classroom, as an example, a classroom may have an ample supply of materials that are organized in conceptually related groups, and children may be observed accessing materials independently (all consistent with Level 4 descriptive indicators), but the classroom's displays may be more teacher-generated than the Level 4 descriptive indicator suggests. In cases such as this one, revisit the anchor statements to guide your scoring. Does the classroom exhibit *sufficient* evidence that the materials are well organized, appealing, accessible, and coordinated with ongoing learning goals? *Some* evidence? *Limited* evidence? Step back from the descriptive indicators and focus on the qualitative anchor statement. Use the evidence you have noted to make your final score determination.

Avoiding Bias

When taking evidence and scoring each particular item, it is important to remain focused on the evidence associated with that item. It is easy for scoring decisions to become clouded by overall impressions of the classroom. A well-stocked and smoothly managed classroom with pleasant teacher–child interactions may predispose an observer to assign higher scores for all of the items, even though there may not be sufficient evidence of effort to build children's vocabulary or engage in extended conversations. Conversely, a teacher with a disorganized classroom may do a wonderful job with book reading and supporting children's writing, but the observer's view may be negatively influenced by the haphazard classroom environment.

Another factor to guard against during scoring is personal bias. Everyone has opinions of what constitutes a good classroom or teacher. Some of these opinions may coincide with the research-based evidence represented in the ELLCO Pre-K items, but other opinions may be irrelevant and solely based on personal preference. The scoring of each item must be based on how the evidence compares with the rubric. It is the observer's job to guard against allowing personal bias to prejudice scoring decisions.

THE TEACHER INTERVIEW

The Teacher Interview portion of the ELLCO Pre-K is designed to provide information to supplement your observation. Interviews should be conducted after you have concluded your observation and during a time when the teacher is free of teaching responsibilities. When you schedule your observation, ask the teacher to set aside time for this brief conversation.

The purpose of the Teacher Interview is twofold. First, the interview allows the observer to gain an understanding of whether the classroom day observed was typical, as indicated by the first question and its probes. This question may become important if the number of children present during the observation differs significantly from the number reported by the teacher prior to your observation. In this way, the observer could determine whether a second visit is required. Second, observers such as supervisors and coaches may be using the ELLCO Pre-K as part of an ongoing professional development initiative. In these cases, the additional teacher interview questions help to illuminate teachers' thinking and planning.

Since the interview provides only supplemental information, teacher responses should not be used as direct evidence for scoring determinations. During the interview, a teacher may confirm what you have already observed, thereby increasing your confidence in assigning a particular rating. On the other hand, if the teacher's interview responses contradict what you observed, you should rely on what you saw and noted during your observation to assign the score.

COMPLETING THE SCORE FORM

The ELLCO Pre-K Score Form provides space to organize the scores for all 19 of the observed items, allows you to calculate subtotals for each section, and enables you to create two overarching subscale scores, one for the general class-room environment and another specifically for language and literacy.

The 19 ELLCO Pre-K items are organized into five sections: Classroom Structure, Curriculum, The Language Environment, Books and Book Reading, and Print and Early Writing. After entering the scores for each item in the blank space provided, you can calculate each section's subtotal by taking the sum of all of the items in the section. The highest possible subtotal for each section is as follows:

- Section I: Classroom Structure (sum of Items 1–4) = 20 points

- Section II: Curriculum (sum of Items 5–7) = 15 points

- Section III: The Language Environment (sum of Items 8–11) = 20 points

- Section IV: Books and Book Reading (sum of Items 12–16) = 25 points

- Section V: Print and Early Writing (sum of Items 17–19) = 15 points

After calculating a subtotal for each of the five sections, you are ready to calculate the two ELLCO Pre-K subscales, the *General Classroom Environment* subscale and the *Language and Literacy* subscale. The subscales can be helpful both as a means of structuring feedback to classroom teachers regarding the results from classroom observations and also to measure changes in these two distinct areas. Subscales are arrived at by combining sections as follows:

Section I: Classroom Structure + Section II: Curriculum = *General Classroom Environment* subscale (35 points total)

Section III: The Language Environment + Section IV: Books and Book Reading + Section V: Print and Early Writing = *Language and Literacy Environment* subscale (60 points total)

In order to derive a level of proficiency for the classroom when tracking sub-scales, the observer simply needs to divide the total points assigned for the sub-scale by the number of items included in it (*General Classroom Environment* subscale = 7; *Language and Literacy Environment* subscale = 12). This will provide an average rating between 1 and 5, generally corresponding to the rating level key words (e.g., Level 4, *strong*). For example, the *Language and Literacy Environment* subscale shown in Figure 4.2 received a total of 43 points of a possible score of 60 points, divided as follows:

The Language Environment Subtotal = 12 points

Books and Book Reading Subtotal = 21 points

Print and Early Writing Subtotal = 10 points

Figure 4.2. Example of a completed ELLCO Pre-K Score Form.

The subscale score (43) divided by number of items in the subscale (12) equals an average score of 3.58. This classroom at this point in time is solidly between *basic* and *strong* for *Language and Literacy Environment* items. By examining the components of the subscale, you can identify particular areas of strength and weakness. In this example, Books and Book Reading is a relative strength (4.2), whereas The Language Environment (3.0) and Print and Early Writing (3.3) are weaker. This type of score analysis allows the ability to track progress over time and to target professional development efforts.

A Review of Sample Items

RECORDING EVIDENCE

Evaluating the quality of evidence is essential to scoring ELLCO Pre-K items. Rating accuracy depends on observers noticing and recording ample descriptive evidence relevant to each item. The ELLCO Pre-K provides space for documenting the observation and includes key words and phrases that focus the observer's attention on sources of evidence. For example, to record evidence for Item 8, observers should note the specific details of verbal interactions, including who is participating, the topic, the duration, the affect of teachers and children, and strategies used to facilitate participation and extend interaction (see Figure 5.1). Due to the nature of this item (e.g., based on conversations), it is often helpful to transcribe segments of interaction verbatim in order to capture the flavor and details of the discourse. It is also important to remember that evidence can be recorded in several places (for instance, a stimulating conversation during book reading might yield evidence for Item 16, Quality of Book Reading; Item 5, Approaches to Curriculum; and Item 8, Discourse Climate). However, the evidence for each must be specifically related to the key elements of the item rated.

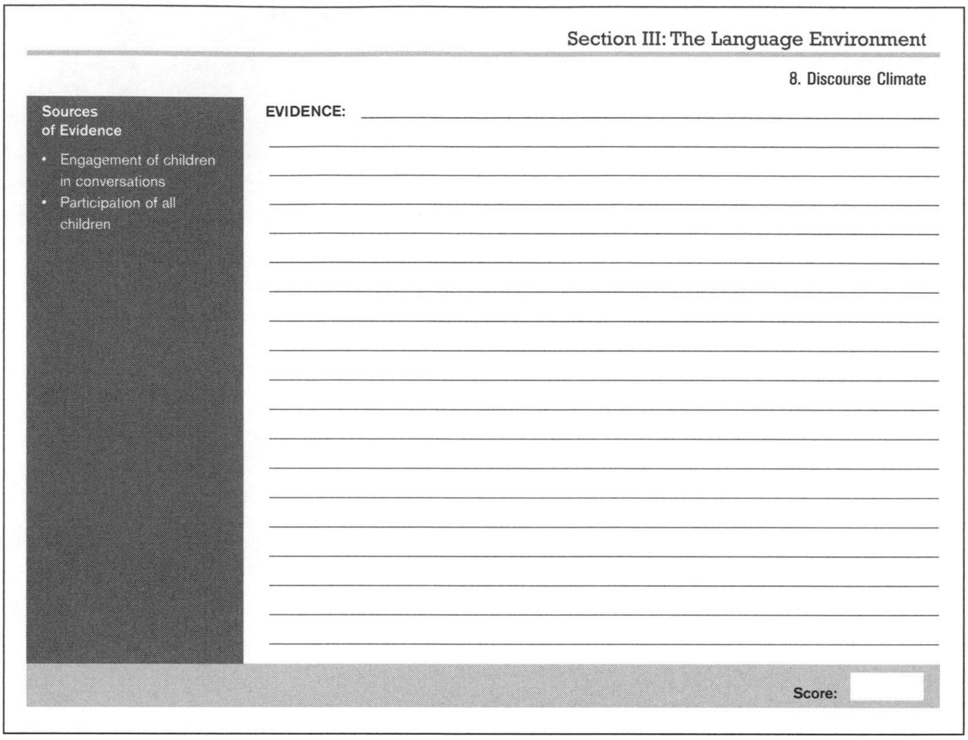

Section III: The Language Environment

8. Discourse Climate

Sources
of Evidence

• Engagement of children
  in conversations
• Participation of all
  children

EVIDENCE: _____

_____

_____

_____

_____

_____

_____

_____

_____

_____

_____

_____

_____

_____

_____

_____

_____

_____

_____

Score: [   ]

Figure 5.1.   Evidence page for ELLCO Pre-K Item 8, Discourse Climate.

UNDERSTANDING THE RUBRICS

Each observation item consists of a rubric with five levels. The anchor statement at each level is most important and should be used as the primary basis for making a scoring decision (see Figure 5.2).

Reading *across* the levels, notice that the phrasing at each level is identical, except for the qualitative words that describe the strength of the evidence (e.g., *exemplary* and *compelling* at Level 5, *strong* and *sufficient* at Level 4).

Reading *within* each level, notice that the anchor statement is followed by a series of bulleted statements that are called descriptive indicators. These *do not* constitute a checklist but are provided to describe in more detail the characteristics of the evidence that might be seen at each scale point (see Figure 5.2).

In order to rate an item, observers must be familiar with the characteristics of the rubric at each scale point and able to make qualitative, differential judgments based on what they saw, heard, and recorded. In learning to use the observation tool, it is helpful to notice what changes from level to level.

What changes from Level 5 to Level 4 (see Figure 5.3)? The quality of the evidence observed shifts from *exemplary* and *compelling* to *strong* and *suffi-*

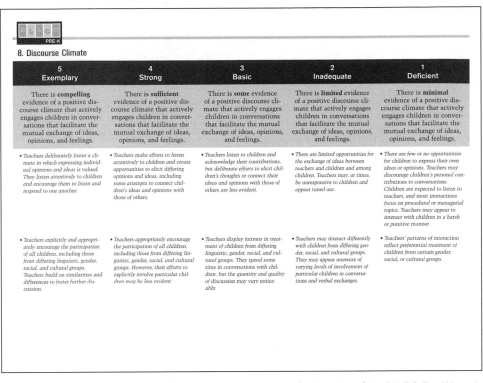

Figure 5.2. Anchor statements (top) and descriptive indicators (bulleted items) for ELLCO Pre-K Item 8, Discourse Climate.

cient. As the descriptive indicators suggest, the teachers may make fewer or weaker efforts to engage multiple children in positive, shared conversations that connect thoughts and ideas, but there are still numerous appropriate and positive interactions. Evidence that teachers work to involve all children and deliberately foster further discussion among children is also present but less notable at Level 4 than at Level 5.

What changes from Level 4 to Level 3 (see Figure 5.4)? The quality of what is observed again shifts downward, this time from *strong* and *sufficient* to *basic* and *some*. Indicators at Level 3 describe generally positive interactions that fairly accept and acknowledge children's contributions; however, strategies do not appear to intentionally engage children in making connections with one another's thoughts and ideas.

What changes from Level 3 to Level 2 (see Figure 5.5)? At Level 2, the quality of the evidence is characterized as *inadequate* and *limited*. Descriptive indicators suggest that, at a Level 2 scale point, the discourse climate may constrain children's interest and ability to participate actively and effectively in exchanges of ideas and information.

Again, the descriptive indicators change from Level 2 (*inadequate* and *limited*) to Level 1 (*deficient* and *minimal*) (see Figure 5.6). Level 1 is characterized

5 Exemplary	4 Strong
There is **compelling** evidence of a positive discourse climate that actively engages children in conversations that facilitate the mutual exchange of ideas, opinions, and feelings.	There is **sufficient** evidence of a positive discourse climate that actively engages children in conversations that facilitate the mutual exchange of ideas, opinions, and feelings.
• *Teachers deliberately foster a climate in which expressing individual opinions and ideas is valued. They listen attentively to children and encourage them to listen and respond to one another.*	• *Teachers make efforts to listen attentively to children and create opportunities to elicit differing opinions and ideas, including some attempts to connect children's ideas and opinions with those of others.*
• *Teachers explicitly and appropriately encourage the participation of all children, including those from differing linguistic, gender, racial, and cultural groups. Teachers build on similarities and differences to foster further discussion.*	• *Teachers appropriately encourage the participation of all children, including those from differing linguistic, gender, racial, and cultural groups. However, their efforts to explicitly involve particular children may be less evident.*

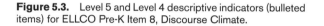

Figure 5.3. Level 5 and Level 4 descriptive indicators (bulleted items) for ELLCO Pre-K Item 8, Discourse Climate.

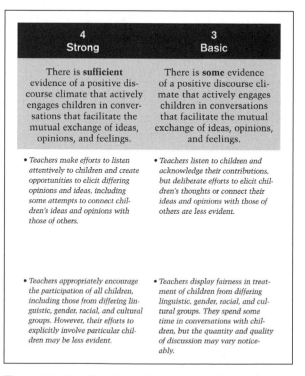

4 Strong	3 Basic
There is **sufficient** evidence of a positive discourse climate that actively engages children in conversations that facilitate the mutual exchange of ideas, opinions, and feelings.	There is **some** evidence of a positive discourse climate that actively engages children in conversations that facilitate the mutual exchange of ideas, opinions, and feelings.
• *Teachers make efforts to listen attentively to children and create opportunities to elicit differing opinions and ideas, including some attempts to connect children's ideas and opinions with those of others.*	• *Teachers listen to children and acknowledge their contributions, but deliberate efforts to elicit children's thoughts or connect their ideas and opinions with those of others are less evident.*
• *Teachers appropriately encourage the participation of all children, including those from differing linguistic, gender, racial, and cultural groups. However, their efforts to explicitly involve particular children may be less evident.*	• *Teachers display fairness in treatment of children from differing linguistic, gender, racial, and cultural groups. They spend some time in conversations with children, but the quantity and quality of discussion may vary noticeably.*

Figure 5.4. Level 4 and Level 3 descriptive indicators (bulleted items) for ELLCO Pre-K Item 8, Discourse Climate.

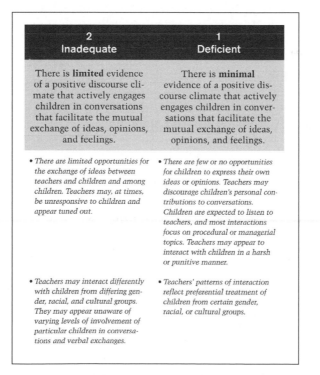

3 Basic	2 Inadequate
There is **some** evidence of a positive discourse climate that actively engages children in conversations that facilitate the mutual exchange of ideas, opinions, and feelings.	There is **limited** evidence of a positive discourse climate that actively engages children in conversations that facilitate the mutual exchange of ideas, opinions, and feelings.
• *Teachers listen to children and acknowledge their contributions, but deliberate efforts to elicit children's thoughts or connect their ideas and opinions with those of others are less evident.*	• *There are limited opportunities for the exchange of ideas between teachers and children and among children. Teachers may, at times, be unresponsive to children and appear tuned out.*
• *Teachers display fairness in treatment of children from differing linguistic, gender, racial, and cultural groups. They spend some time in conversations with children, but the quantity and quality of discussion may vary noticeably.*	• *Teachers may interact differently with children from differing gender, racial, and cultural groups. They may appear unaware of varying levels of involvement of particular children in conversations and verbal exchanges.*

Figure 5.5. Level 3 and Level 2 descriptive indicators (bulleted items) for ELLCO Pre-K Item 8, Discourse Climate.

2 Inadequate	1 Deficient
There is **limited** evidence of a positive discourse climate that actively engages children in conversations that facilitate the mutual exchange of ideas, opinions, and feelings.	There is **minimal** evidence of a positive discourse climate that actively engages children in conversations that facilitate the mutual exchange of ideas, opinions, and feelings.
• *There are limited opportunities for the exchange of ideas between teachers and children and among children. Teachers may, at times, be unresponsive to children and appear tuned out.*	• *There are few or no opportunities for children to express their own ideas or opinions. Teachers may discourage children's personal contributions to conversations. Children are expected to listen to teachers, and most interactions focus on procedural or managerial topics. Teachers may appear to interact with children in a harsh or punitive manner.*
• *Teachers may interact differently with children from differing gender, racial, and cultural groups. They may appear unaware of varying levels of involvement of particular children in conversations and verbal exchanges.*	• *Teachers' patterns of interaction reflect preferential treatment of children from certain gender, racial, or cultural groups.*

Figure 5.6. Level 2 and Level 1 descriptive indicators (bulleted items) for ELLCO Pre-K Item 8, Discourse Climate.

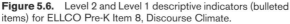

by a discourse climate that severely restricts children's ability to participate and indicates patterns of unfair, unacceptable favoritism for some children.

FROM EVIDENCE TO RUBRIC TO RATING

In order to make a final score determination, the observer must consider the evidence taken in light of the rubric for each item.

Example 1: Item 8—Discourse Climate

A sample evidence page from a completed observation form for Item 8, Discourse Climate, is provided in Figure 5.7. In Figure 5.7, below the filled-in page from the ELLCO Pre-K is a recap of pertinent exchanges and events from the observation. Though this is just a brief example, it captures how the teacher leads children to listen to each other's ideas and work through their disagreements toward a mutually agreeable solution ("Hold on, boys. Let's work this out"). She accepts and builds on their different ideas ("strong" versus "tall") to foster joint problem solving that is respectful of each child's contributions. She also reinforces the boys' knowledge of dinosaurs and their skill in working with materials. The fact that the boys so readily reach a solution may indicate their familiarity and comfort with this teacher's approach. Based on the strength of this example, in conjunction with other evidence taken during the observation, this classroom would receive a score of 5 for this item.

Example 2: Item 16—Quality of Book Reading

Evidence for Item 16, Quality of Book Reading, includes observation of a book reading session, the selected book, strategies for comprehension, strategies for engagement, and the expressiveness and fluency with which the teacher reads. Figure 5.8 shows a sample evidence page from a completed observation form and a recap for Item 16.

In this example, the teacher reads to the full group. This is a first reading of a classic children's book (*Peter's Chair*) with text appropriate for preschoolers and including characters (Peter) and themes (a new baby) appealing to children. The teacher appears to have prepared for the reading in advance (sticky notes on some pages, several vocabulary words explained). She accepts children's contributions during the reading and uses the pictures and text to reinforce the vocabulary words she has selected. Although she offers the children

Section III: The Language Environment

8. Discourse Climate

Sources of Evidence
- Engagement of children in conversations
- Participation of all children

EVIDENCE: F.P.—activity ctrs—3 boys in blocks w/dinos, tch nearby @ craft table

B1: "Put it here. Make it strong."   B2: "No!"   B1: "But we need it here (grabs)"

B2: "No" (grabs back)   Tch comes—Hold on, boys! Let's work this out. B1 wants it "strong." B2 wants it "tall."

Tch summarizes: "So Anish wants it strong & Noah wants it tall."

Says "You both know a lot about dinos—strong can push thru well, tall can go over." Asks boys to solve.

B2 gets bigger block, B1 agrees.

Tch: "Now it's tall _and_ strong."

Score: 5

Recap of Evidence

Free play time, students in activity centers

Three boys (B1, B2, and B3) are in the block area, building and placing dinosaur figures in structures, with a teacher (T) nearby. (In the recap shown below, B3 does not speak.)

B1: Put it here. Make it strong.
B2: No!
B1: But we need it here. (B1 grabs.)
B2: No! (B2 grabs back.)
 T: Hold on, boys. Let's work this out. Anish, you want Noah to put the block right there. Can you tell him your idea?
B1: This wall has to be strong so the dinosaurs won't get out.
 T: Okay. Noah, what is your idea?
B2: We have to make it tall.
 T: So, Anish needs it strong, and Noah wants it tall. Sounds to me like you both know a lot about dinosaurs–Anish knows that they are strong and can push through strong walls, and Noah knows that they are tall and can get over short walls. Can you boys figure out a way to make both ideas work?
B2: Let's use this! (B2 gets a larger block.)
B1: Okay!
 T: Now it's tall and strong! Great work coming up with a compromise!

Figure 5.7.   Example of a completed evidence page (top) for ELLCO Pre-K Item 8, Discourse Climate, and a recap of pertinent events from the observation session (bottom).

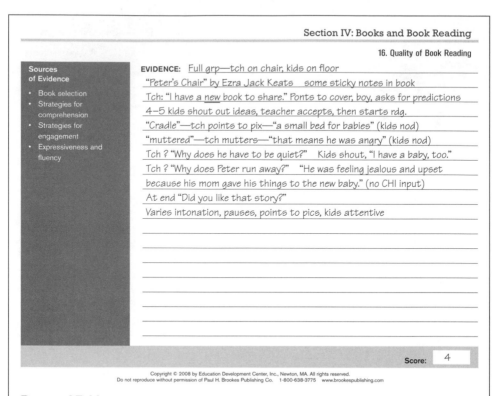

Section IV: Books and Book Reading

16. Quality of Book Reading

Sources of Evidence

• Book selection
• Strategies for comprehension
• Strategies for engagement
• Expressiveness and fluency

EVIDENCE: Full grp—tch on chair, kids on floor

"Peter's Chair" by Ezra Jack Keats   some sticky notes in book

Tch: "I have a new book to share." Ponts to cover, boy, asks for predictions

4–5 kids shout out ideas, teacher accepts, then starts rdg.

"Cradle"—tch points to pix—"a small bed for babies" (kids nod)

"muttered"—tch mutters—"that means he was angry" (kids nod)

Tch ? "Why does he have to be quiet?"   Kids shout, "I have a baby, too."

Tch ? "Why does Peter run away?"   "He was feeling jealous and upset

because his mom gave his things to the new baby." (no CHI input)

At end "Did you like that story?"

Varies intonation, pauses, points to pics, kids attentive

Score: 4

Recap of Evidence

Full-group reading of *Peter's Chair* by Ezra Jack Keats. First reading of book; teacher tells group that she has a new book to share with them. Reads the title, author and illustrator; explains that Ezra Jack Keats wrote the words and drew the pictures. Evidence of planning; teacher has some sticky notes on pages of book. Gives a brief introduction to the book; tells group that the boy on cover is named Peter, and asks them, "What do you think might happen to Peter in the story?" She allows a few (four to five) children to respond and then moves on with reading. Teacher varies intonation and pace; children stay interested and focused throughout reading. During the reading teacher points out some key vocabulary words, describes *cradle* as a small bed for babies and demonstrates, and explains the word *muttered:* "That means he was angry." At one point she asks, "Why does Peter have to be quiet?" Some children shout out that they have a baby at home too. Teacher allows these children to share their ideas, but doesn't connect their comments back to the story. Later in the story she asks, "Why does Peter run away?" and then comments, "He was feeling jealous and upset because his mom gave his things to the new baby." At the end of the story the teacher asks, "Did you like that story about Peter?"

Figure 5.8. Example of a completed evidence page (top) for ELLCO Pre-K Item 16, Quality of Book Reading, and a recap of pertinent events from the observation session (bottom).

an appropriate analysis of the central idea of the story (e.g., jealousy) that supports their comprehension, the teacher does not use children's input as a means to build understanding of ideas central to the story. The teacher reads with fluency and variation in expression that holds children's interest and asks for their evaluation at the conclusion of the story ("Did you like that?").

In order to rate this item or any other, observers should begin at Level 5. Because of the strength of the evidence noted for this section, the rating decision requires considering a Level 5 versus a Level 4. This was a strong, engaging book reading that moved beyond a basic level (see Figure 5.9). Reaching a decision requires balancing the specific evidence in relation to the descriptive indicators and referring back to the anchor statements of the rubric. Although the first indicator is the same for the two levels, the subsequent ones differentiate. In this case, a preponderance of the evidence falls within the Level 4. The teacher accepts children's contributions but does not use them to build understanding and thinking. The teacher supplies an analysis of the main theme of the story rather than encouraging children to offer their own analyses. In addition, the teacher uses expressiveness and fluency to hold children's interest. In sum, the evidence for this item leads to a final score of 4, *strong* and *sufficient*.

5 Exemplary	4 Strong
There is **compelling** evidence that teachers thoughtfully selected the book, prepared for the session, and conducted an engaging reading and discussion to promote learning.	There is **sufficient** evidence that teachers thoughtfully selected the book, prepared for the session, and conducted an engaging reading and discussion to promote learning.
• *The book selected is at an appropriate level of difficulty and includes high-quality text and content of interest to young children.*	• *The book selected is at an appropriate level of difficulty and includes high-quality text and content of interest to young children.*
• *Advanced planning and preparation are evident in the nature of the questions and comments posed by teachers. Questions and comments consistently foster children's interest and comprehension. Children's contributions are encouraged and used to build their understanding of the book and their thinking.*	• *Advanced planning and preparation are evident in the nature of the questions and comments posed by teachers. Questions and comments foster children's interest and comprehension. Children's contributions are acknowledged and valued.*
• *Teachers attend to features of text, pictures, and ideas during the book reading to encourage children's active engagement with the content of the book and to support their comprehension.*	• *Teachers attend to features of the text and pictures to encourage children's comprehension of the book.*
• *Teachers' reading is characterized by expressiveness and fluency, which support children's understanding of the book, characters, and/or content.*	• *Teachers use expressiveness and fluency to hold children's attention and interest during the book-reading session.*

Figure 5.9. Level 5 and Level 4 descriptive indicators (bulleted items) for ELLCO Pre-K Item 16, Quality of Book Reading.

Example 3: Item 17—Early Writing Environment

Evidence for Item 17, Early Writing Environment, is derived from observations of strategies to motivate children to write and to create opportunities for writing. Further, this item considers the nature of materials available to children for writing and the extent and quality of children's and teachers' writing that is displayed around the room. A sample evidence page for Item 17, along with a recap of the observation, is shown in Figure 5.10.

Section V: Print and Early Writing

17. Early Writing Environment

Sources of Evidence

• Motivation and opportunity to write
• Materials
• Examples of writing

EVIDENCE: Writing center—adjacent to book area

Table, 4 chairs, shelves, papers, pencils, markers, scissors, alphabet strip, animal stencils, & stamps (?)

Tch: "Don't forget your name on that." Child writes own name

Drawing/wrtg hung up around room—some scribbles, some names, one picture w/tch labels "mom, me, dad" below figures

Score: 3

Recap of Evidence

Separate writing center included in the classroom; located near book area. Writing center includes a table with chairs for four children and a well-organized shelf stocked with a variety of materials: markers, pencils, colored pencils, and a variety of paper (unlined, lined, small notebook size). Alphabet strip is taped onto table. Also there are animal stencils, animal rubber stamps, and scissors. Teachers remind children to put their names on their drawings and stencil work at the writing center. A teacher asks children to bring a marker over to the easel so that she can write children's names on their paintings. No writing materials are included in other areas. Children's individual drawings, some with scribbling and attempts at name writing are hung on the sides of the shelf by the writing center and in random places in the classroom, by the bathroom, and on the wall by the door. One drawing has labels written by a teacher with the words *mom, me,* and *dad.*

Figure 5.10.   Example of a completed evidence page (top) for ELLCO Pre-K Item 17, Early Writing Environment, and a recap of pertinent events from the observation session (bottom).

In this example, the observer provides both an inventory of the items included in the classroom writing center as well as examples of the ways in which children and teachers use writing in the classroom. There is a separate writing area that contains a variety of materials and motivations for children's work, though there are few models of teachers' writing. The examples of children's writing seen around the room include basic purposes of naming and labeling, and during the observation the teacher labels children's artwork and encourages them to do the same (see Figure 5.11).

In this case, initial review of the evidence would lead an observer to consider Level 4, Level 3, and Level 2 anchor statements and descriptive indicators. The evidence is clearly not *compelling*, so Level 5 is not considered. There might, however, be *sufficient*, *some*, or *limited* evidence, depending on the specific characteristics of the evidence noted. Once again, the trained observer must analyze the rubric at each level and consider the evidence. There is a separate writing area that contains varied and appropriate materials, and some motivational materials for children's writing (e.g., alphabet, small notepads), which

4 Strong	3 Basic	2 Inadequate
There is **sufficient** evidence that writing materials and displays encourage children's awareness of print and the varied purposes of writing.	There is **some** evidence that writing materials and displays encourage children's awareness of print and the varied purposes of writing.	There is **limited** evidence that writing materials and displays encourage children's awareness of print and the varied purposes of writing.
• *Opportunities are provided within the classroom for children to use their emergent writing skills although the opportunities may be less integrated and somewhat less motivating. Writing is clearly differentiated from art activities.*	• *Opportunities are provided within the classroom for children to see writing and to use their emergent writing skills. The motivations for children's writing include basic functions such as naming and labeling.*	• *Opportunities may be provided within the classroom for children to use their emergent writing skills, but the purpose and appeal of these activities is narrowly defined and the motivation unclear.*
• *There are varied and appropriate materials and tools available in a designated writing area. Some additional writing props may be available in other areas of the classroom, such as the block area and/or dramatic play area.*	• *Appropriate materials are available for children to use for writing activities. These might include writing implements, paper, and envelopes in a designated area of the classroom or at the writing table. In classrooms where writing materials and art supplies are combined, children are observed using materials to write simple names or words.*	• *Materials are not specifically designated for purposeful writing activities and may be primarily related to art areas and activities (e.g., markers available to write names or labels on paintings).*
• *There are examples of the written word (e.g., children's work, teacher-generated text, commercially produced materials) that exemplify varied purposes of writing.*	• *Examples of the written word are evident and may include children's work, though there may be less variety and less obvious connection between the displays and varied purposes of writing.*	• *Examples of the written word are mostly teacher-generated or commercial products that do not convey a sense of the varied purposes of writing.*

Figure 5.11.   Levels 4, 3, and 2 descriptive indicators (bulleted items) for ELLCO Pre-K Item 17, Early Writing Environment.

distinguishes the evidence from the Level 2 category. There are a few examples of some of the functions of writing seen around the room and in teacher–child exchanges (e.g., labels, names on papers). There do not appear to be writing materials and strategies or activities to motivate writing in other areas of the classroom. Nor are there multiple examples of the written word that exemplify varied purposes of writing, distinguishing the evidence from the Level 4 category. In sum, the evidence leads to a score determination of 3 (*basic*).

6

Using the ELLCO Pre-K for Professional Development

The ELLCO Pre-K offers practitioners a vision for evidence-based practices that support children's language and literacy development in the early years. The structure of the instrument is explicitly designed—through the use of carefully crafted descriptive indicators—to provide a continuum that can help teachers see where they are now and where they want to go. Accordingly, the ELLCO Pre-K can be used as an effective professional development tool to help teachers build their understanding of the essential features of early language and literacy practice to enhance their own classrooms.

Early child care and education programs engage in many types of professional development activities. Those that are carried out over time, employ multiple support strategies, and engage teachers as active participants in the planning and assessment have been found to lead to more sustained, positive changes (Dickinson & Brady, 2006; Landry, Swank, Smith, & Assel, 2006). Whatever your staff development design may be, the ELLCO Pre-K can supplement your efforts in multiple ways. For instance, in Head Start programs using literacy coaches, the tool can be used to make initial assessments and track changes over time. In such cases, the ELLCO Pre-K offers a common set of practices that teachers and coaches together can use to note progress and identify areas that require more attention.

Other early childhood programs are adopting the study-group approach as an alternative to more traditional workshops. In such settings, teachers gather regularly to explore a common issue relevant to their practice, sometimes orchestrated by a supervisor or content specialist. The ELLCO Pre-K can serve as a basis for organizing such professional conversations when the topic is early literacy. By using various sections of the tool (e.g., Books and Book Reading) as a springboard for discussion and the exchange of ideas, the ELLCO Pre-K can be a practical aid in teacher development. Below, we suggest specific ideas about how to incorporate the ELLCO Pre-K into efforts to strengthen the quality of language and literacy practices in center-based early childhood classrooms for 3- to 5-year-olds.

TIPS FOR INCORPORATING THE ELLCO PRE-K INTO LANGUAGE AND LITERACY PRACTICES

Step 1: Create a Positive Climate for Teacher Development

Your work as a professional development specialist or supervisor is parallel to that of teachers. Just as teachers seek to create positive, stimulating learning environments for children, so also do supervisors and others concerned with teacher development. Teachers in early childhood have become increasingly sensitive to assessment instruments as a means of monitoring their compliance and performance. Therefore, from the start it is vital to introduce the ELLCO Pre-K as a way to stimulate thinking about practice rather than as a summative appraisal of performance. To create a safe environment for teachers' reflection and motivation to learn, consider the following suggestions:

- Begin by engaging in a discussion with teachers about their own goals for growth and learning. Ask them what they hope to learn, and probe for areas of strength and accomplishment.

- Clarify the role you expect to play in the professional development and your partnership in the learning process. If you are supervising the teachers you are working with, underscore how your role in professional development is distinct from your regular oversight.

- Emphasize that the process inherent in becoming a reflective practitioner is at its core developmental in nature. Stress that change happens over time—for teachers as well as children.

- Keep the focus on children's learning and engagement. Describe ways that the ELLCO Pre-K can be used to understand complex features of the classroom that influence children's language and literacy development.

- Make your own intentions transparent. Articulate your goals for using the ELLCO Pre-K in the professional development process by describing why you have selected it and how you will use it. Reinforce the ways that teachers are integral to the process and encourage them to become critical observers of their own practices.

Step 2: Preview the ELLCO Together

Both the tool itself and the *ELLCO Pre-K User's Guide* contain a wealth of relevant information that can help teachers develop a vision of exemplary practices and understand the research base. The guide also presents many teacher-friendly resources that can be used in a range of creative ways. What is important is that you encourage teachers to view the materials directly but discuss them together. Some ways to begin your collaborative review include

- Articulate your goals for using the ELLCO Pre-K in this process, describing why you have selected it and how you will use it. Reinforce that teachers' engagement is essential since a critical element of success is their ability to become critical assessors of their own practices.

- Read and discuss Chapter 2, "Effective Elements of Early Literacy: Kendra's Story," which provides vignettes that describe how a child's experiences in a preschool classroom can enrich language and literacy development. Consider posing questions after each vignette to provoke thinking about Miss Rosa's and Miss Denise's roles in bringing about Kendra's actions and reactions. Discuss the implications of each vignette for practice. Highlight those areas that tie to teachers' own goals for professional development.

- Use Kendra's Story as a deliberate vehicle for becoming familiar with the ELLCO Pre-K. Initially, the rubrics for rating items (Levels 5 through 1) that are used in the tool can be overwhelming to early childhood teachers who are unaccustomed to using such guides to assess student work; this strategy is more common in upper elementary grades and beyond. Appearing after each vignette in Kendra's Story is a list of ELLCO Pre-K items that could be rated in part when considering each snapshot of teaching and learning. Introducing the items and the rubric in such a measured way may make the tool more accessible to many early childhood teachers.

- Review the range of resources listed at the end of the book, including a comprehensive list of web sites, web-based resources, books, and articles germane to early language and literacy classroom practices. Selected for their relevance at different levels of sophistication, these materials can provide teachers with information about evidence-based practices as well as concrete assistance such as selecting books for their classroom. Take time to identify specific resources that map on to teachers' professional goals and bring them to their attention.

- Read and discuss examples of items and ratings from this user's guide. If the whole tool seems overwhelming at first, settle on one or two of the five sections for an initial focus. Help teachers decode the rubric for rating each item. One way to get teachers accustomed to the rubric language is to have them highlight the areas that are different for each descriptive indicator, moving from Level 5 (*exemplary*) across the scale to Level 1 (*deficient*), in the same manner observers would to prepare for an observation.

Step 3: Conduct an Initial Observation

The ELLCO Pre-K can be used flexibly for professional development purposes. For example, you might choose to complete just one section per observation or focus on a limited number of items that are most important to a particular teacher or classroom. Observing in classrooms can be rewarding and challenging. Follow the guidelines for observation in Chapter 4, "How to Conduct an ELLCO Pre-K Observation" to ensure that you are as fair and impartial as possible.

- Be sure to set up a mutually agreeable time for an initial observation. Consider the teacher's goals and select a time and a day when the teacher will be engaged directly with children in activities likely to provide fruitful material for a post-observation debriefing. Also arrange a time when you can meet to discuss the observation. It is usually difficult to debrief immediately after the observation, but it is critical to discuss it soon—preferably on the same day—otherwise the events will lose their freshness, especially for the teacher.

- Take plenty of notes that will serve as evidence of what you see and hear during your observation. Evidence not only helps you decide on a rating, it also provides the concrete examples that will form the basis of your post-observation conversation with the teacher. The more detailed and specific the notes, the more effective you can be in providing thoughtful feedback.

- Maintain an unobtrusive presence in the classroom while observing. Pay particular attention to preserving a neutral expression, despite what you might see or hear. Teachers will be anxious to get your quick, "sound bite" feedback before you leave, so be prepared. You might simply say, "Thanks for letting me observe. I enjoyed it and appreciated seeing you read *Silly Sally*. I'll see you at the end of the day."

- Many coaches use videotape as a tool in professional development. To ensure a stable picture with good-quality sound, it is important to use a tripod and a microphone that will pick up what the teacher and children say. It is most effective to focus the videotaping on a particular activity, for instance, a full-group book reading. Use the videotaped footage as the basis for debriefing with the teacher.

Step 4: Share Results

For many literacy coaches and supervisors, sharing the results of an ELLCO Pre-K observation can be intimidating. Here are some strategies for structuring feedback conversations in ways that are positive and supportive and that lead toward productive goal-setting.

- Remind the teacher that this initial observation is to be used as the basis for a beginning conversation about what is currently happening in the classroom and to generate goals for changing and improving practices.

- Remind yourself and the teacher of the big picture you are both working toward, to provide opportunities and experiences for young children that support their learning in multiple areas of development, with particular consideration given to language and literacy learning.

- Ask the teacher for his or her perspective first. Be prepared to probe and wait if the teacher feels reluctant. Many teachers equate their reflection on what happened to criticism. Some, therefore, only discuss what was problematic. Others, who may be reticent to indicate that they were pleased with the outcome, may say nothing at all. You can assist teachers unaccustomed to reflecting on practice by modeling an approach. In the face of silence, you can *briefly* recap an event observed, probing for the teacher's assessment of children's engagement. What is essential is that the teacher, not you, be the main contributor to the conversation. Avoid filling the silence with your own assessment.

- If you are videotaping your observation, find a time to review the videotape before meeting with the teacher, noting your questions and feedback. At the debriefing, view the footage with the teacher, making sure you use the aforementioned strategies to elicit the teacher's reactions first.

- As much as possible, link your own feedback to the teacher's comments. Begin by sharing some positive points from your observation, then move into reviewing specific items and ratings. Remember to emphasize strengths and couple comments about weaknesses with suggestions for alternative approaches.

Step 5: Generate Goals

Based on one or more observations and debriefings, you should have a good baseline understanding of the starting point and even preliminary goals for professional development. Setting goals is an iterative process; as you and teachers become more comfortable in this mentoring relationship, goals will be refined and expanded. When setting goals,

- Begin with some concrete areas that are more easily influenced. If there is little or no early writing happening by design, begin with a focus on the writing environment. Establish a writing center; review some resources that list ideas for supplies. Move steadily toward ideas that require more substantive change, such as the curriculum and instructional approach.

- Use the ELLCO Pre-K descriptive indicators as a way to prompt teachers to articulate their own criteria for success. At the same time that you are building teachers' knowledge and skill in early literacy, you also are promoting the development of reflective practitioners.

- Establish a reasonable timeframe for change. Some teachers tend to be overly ambitious about how quickly they can adopt new practices and consequently get discouraged when it takes longer than originally anticipated. Inject some realism and analysis to balance the initial enthusiasm that you may encounter. Remember that concrete environmental changes are easier to implement than those that require modifications in interaction and instruction.

BEGINNING STEPS TOWARD CHANGE

The overall goal of professional development is to build a cadre of reflective early childhood practitioners who are intentional in what they teach and how they teach it. Such teachers are constantly engaged in refining their skills and assessing their own effectiveness in light of children's development and learning. The ELLCO Pre-K can play a significant role in transforming practice, but it will be most effective if used as a part of an ongoing, coherent system of quality improvement and professional development. The ideas presented below are offered to help supervisors, literacy coaches, and others tie their support activities to the five sections of the ELLCO Pre-K.

Section I: Classroom Structure (Organization, Contents, Management, Personnel)

Beginning with an analysis of the physical environment is typically a comfortable, concrete way for teachers to begin to reflect on the what, why, and how of their classrooms. Some ways to encourage analysis might include

- Mapping the layout of the classroom (Why are particular interest areas and furnishings placed where they are? What considerations go into an effective classroom layout?)

- Observing and mapping patterns of traffic flow (How do children and teachers actually use the space? Are there areas of congestion? Do unused areas exist?)

- Listing classroom areas and their intended uses

- Conducting an inventory of materials in the classroom

- Observing and recording children's actual use of classroom areas

- Listing or creating a running record of adult roles

- Tracking time spent in management activities and conversations

- Tracking time spent in transitions

Section II: Curriculum (Approaches, Child Choice, Diversity)

Facilitating children's development and learning through curriculum includes many facets, and the curriculum section of the ELLCO Pre-K delineates several areas for consideration. Structuring the classroom day, determining the themes and topics to be studied, and attending to the diverse needs of individual learners within the context of daily classroom life are challenges for most teachers. Here are some ways to begin thinking about these intertwined strands:

- Look critically at patterns of time use, scheduling, and grouping in the classroom, analyzing the amount and quality of time spent in varied settings, groupings, and activities connected to learning.

- List curriculum topics and themes, describing general and specific learning goals and activities that relate to those goals.

- Observe, note, and analyze areas of diversity among classroom members; in addition to more obvious characteristics, this might also include considering diverse approaches to learning (e.g., Jacob learns best when he can use his entire body; Lucy prefers to observe before joining).

- Brainstorm approaches to curriculum planning that capitalize on the diversity of the group and the strengths and needs of individuals, then try out curriculum plans and ideas, assessing strengths and areas for improvement.

Section III: The Language Environment (Discourse Climate, Extended Conversations, Vocabulary, Phonological Awareness)

The items in this section of the ELLCO Pre-K are derived from extensive research that has pinpointed specific characteristics of talk that build children's language skills. The items are organized from the more general Discourse Climate to the more specific Phonological Awareness. For many teachers, becoming aware of their own language use with children is, in itself, an eye-opening experience that leads to reflective analysis and reconsideration of their tone, conversational topics, and use of vocabulary. Here are some ways to begin this process:

- Tape record interactions in the classroom and analyze them for substance and turn-taking.

- Brainstorm familiar and new topics and associated challenging vocabulary (e.g., concept webbing, KWL [What I Know, What I Want to Know, What I Have Learned], research).

- Generate initial questions, comments, or activities that might provoke children's interest in a topic, along with ideas for introducing vocabulary.

- Learn and implement strategies to promote phonological awareness (playful rhyming, alliteration, sound play).

Section IV: Books (Organization, Characteristics of Books, Books for Learning)

One of the best and easiest ways for children to become effective users of language, and eventually to become readers and writers, is through using and listening to books. The book-related items on the ELLCO Pre-K delineate a variety of ways in which books can be used to facilitate and extend children's learning. How and where in the classroom books are organized, displayed, and used is important to consider, along with characteristics of the books themselves. Below are some ways to begin thinking about the presence and use of books.

- Assess the location of the classroom book area and how it is currently used by children and teachers.

- Conduct an inventory of books and an analysis of their characteristics along varied dimensions (e.g., condition, difficulty of text, range of topics, quality of illustrations, diversity of genres and characters).

- List classroom interest areas and generate ideas for how books might be meaningfully incorporated within them.

- Develop plans to actively use books in conjunction with children's interests and ongoing curriculum topics and themes.

- Seek out, read aloud, and supply the classroom with a wide range of high-quality children's books.

Section IV: Book Reading (Approaches, Quality)

In addition to characteristics and use of books, the way in which teachers read books to children has been an area of considerable research that is reflected in the book reading items of the ELLCO Pre-K (Dickinson & Smith, 1994; Justice & Kaderavek, 2002; McKeown & Beck, 2006; Snow, Burns, & Griffin, 1998). Next are some ways to begin to help teachers focus on several aspects of their own book-reading practices:

- Think and talk about teachers' own favorite read-aloud books.

- Examine the schedule and the roles of the teaching team to allow for more frequent small-group book reading.

- Tape record or videotape small- or large-group book-reading sessions to review and analyze the quality of reading and children's engagement.

- Preread books to prepare for book reading with children, generate questions and comments in advance of reading, and plan for curriculum extensions related to books selected.

- Explore the differences between a first read of a book in order to maintain the flow of the story and subsequent re-reading to deepen understanding about story structure, characters, and vocabulary.

Section V: Early Writing (Environment, Support, Environmental Print)

Children who are surrounded by multiple and diverse examples of spoken and written language develop a rich understanding of how words work and how print and words are connected. The early writing items (in Section V: Print and

Early Writing) of the ELLCO Pre-K delineate several ways that teachers can structure the classroom environment and their interactions with children to facilitate and support the emerging capacities of their students as readers and writers. Some additional suggestions for looking in detail at early writing opportunities in the classroom follow:

- Analyze the current writing area for varied writing materials and supplies (e.g., types, sizes, and shapes of paper; envelopes; pencils; pens; clipboards), tracking changes in children's use of the area.

- Collect and display samples of children's writing, seeking to understand the purposes of their writing and what messages they are trying to communicate.

- Assess the functional daily uses of writing in the classroom for both teachers (e.g., morning message) and children (e.g., use of a sign-in routine) to build on and expand the ways writing is used.

- Explore the teacher's role in modeling and supporting children's writing (e.g., if you designate one teacher to sit in the writing area and assist children in their writing efforts, what happens?)

- List, discuss, and analyze existing environmental print, brainstorming additional strategies for the inclusion of meaningful environmental print in the classroom.

REFERENCES

Dickinson, D.K., & Brady, J.P. (2006). Toward effective support for language and literacy through professional development. In M. Zaslow & I. Martinez-Beck (Eds.), *Critical issues in early childhood professional development* (pp. 141–170). Baltimore: Paul H. Brookes Publishing Co.

Dickinson, D.K., & Smith, M.W. (1994). Long-term effects of preschool teachers' book readings on low-income children's vocabulary and story comprehension. *Reading Research Quarterly, 29*(2), 104–122.

Justice, L.M., & Kaderavek, J. (2002). Using shared storybook reading to promote emergent literacy. *Teaching Exceptional Children, 34*(4), 8–13.

Landry, S.H., Swank, P.R., Smith, K.E., & Assel, M.A. (2006). Enhancing early literacy skills for preschool children: Bringing a professional development model to scale. *Journal of Learning Disabilities, 39*(4), 306–324.

McKeown, M.G., & Beck, I.L. (2006). Encouraging young children's language interactions with stories. In D.K. Dickinson & S.B. Neuman (Eds.), *Handbook of early literacy research* (Vol. 2, pp. 281–294). New York: Guilford Press.

Snow, C.E., Burns, S.M., & Griffin, P. (Eds.). (1998). *Preventing reading difficulties in young children.* Washington, DC: National Academies Press.

Using the ELLCO Pre-K in Research

Using the ELLCO Pre-K for research requires skilled observers in order to maintain high standards of accuracy. Observers selected to collect data should be familiar with preschool classrooms, have knowledge of early language and literacy, and have classroom observation experience. Even when observers meet all of these criteria, individuals may approach their observations differently because of their unique perspectives and experiences. Because two individuals with similar training can view the same phenomenon differently, there is the potential for measurement error in any observational rating scale. Steps that can be taken to reduce measurement error include training, practicing and calibrating ratings, calculating interrater reliability, and recalibrating ratings while collecting data.

TRAINING

ELLCO Pre-K training provides observers with a common lens through which to view classrooms while conducting their observations. ELLCO Pre-K training consists of a careful review of all of the items and focuses on the evidence associated with each item. Training provides participants with an opportunity to observe and score actual classrooms in order to become familiar with recording the evidence and choosing the appropriate rating. Each opportunity to rate an item should be followed by a conversation with trainers to compare ratings, discuss appropriate scores, and review areas of disagreement. As a result, data collectors leave the training session with a common idea of how to approach observations and assign scores.

PRACTICING AND CALIBRATING RATINGS

In addition to traditional user training, data collectors should practice using the ELLCO Pre-K in several classrooms prior to conducting any observations that will serve as a data point. Conduct these practice sessions in teams or small groups and follow each observation with a debriefing conversation to calibrate ratings. Observers should compare ratings and discuss their rationale for assigning each score based on the evidence noted to support their judgments. These conversations are vital exercises that enable observation teams to come to consensus on difficult scoring decisions. The nature and extent of the evidence recorded are useful ways to gauge an individual's ability to both harvest and represent relevant information during classroom observations. Relying on memory will be problematic, especially when data collectors work across numerous classrooms in a compressed timeframe.

INTERRATER RELIABILITY

In order to be confident that individuals are rating classrooms reliably, observers should conduct joint observations to calculate interrater reliability, or the degree of agreement among raters. Options for calculation of interrater reliability include a simple calculation of the percentage of agreement (the number of items given identical ratings divided by the total number of items) as well as more robust estimates that take into account agreement that might occur by chance such as Cohen's kappa (Cohen, 1960; used when there are two raters) and Fleiss's kappa (Fleiss, 1981; used when there are more than two raters). Landis and Koch (1977) indicated that a kappa of .40–.59 is moderate interrater reliability, a kappa of .60–.79 is substantial, and a kappa of .80 is outstanding. A kappa estimate of .70, however, is generally considered acceptable interrater reliability (Subkoviak, 1988). It is up to the researcher to decide which estimate and level of interrater reliability is appropriate for his or her research study.

RECALIBRATION IN THE FIELD

In most research and evaluation activities, there is substantial time pressure to gather pre- and postintervention data. Once the training of data collectors is complete, often observers are scheduled to visit multiple classrooms in the field, cycling completed forms back to the research team. If observers are left on their own, their ratings can drift over time. Some may become overconfident of their understanding of the rubric and lax about taking evidence and using it against the rubric to settle on a rating. Others may slowly drift to their own heuristic and begin scoring items based on their own rubric, affecting the reliability of the ratings. It is, therefore, advisable to recalibrate data collectors to ensure that they are using the tool correctly. Recalibration with an expert observer should occur approximately at the midpoint of the data collection schedule. Some would advise that it should take place within 2 weeks of the original training. The recalibration process involves scheduling a joint observation (i.e., both the expert observer and data collector) and debriefing afterwards using the same protocols that were put in place during the initial training.

REFERENCES

Cohen, J. (1960). A coefficient of agreement for nominal scales. *Educational and Psychological Measurement, 20,* 37–46.

Fleiss, J.L. (1981). *Statistical methods for rates and proportions* (2nd ed.). New York: John Wiley & Sons.

Landis, J.R., & Koch, G. (1977). The measurement of observer agreement for categorical data. *Biometrics, 33,* 159–174.

Subkoviak, M.J. (1988, Spring). A practitioner's guide to computation and interpretation of reliability indices for mastery tests. *Journal of Educational Measurement, 25*(1), 47–55.

Technical Appendix

This technical appendix reports data that were collected from 1997 to 2002 as part of the development of the ELLCO Toolkit, Research Edition, as well as additional data that were collected from 2002 to 2007 using the Research Edition. As described in Chapter 1, on the basis of this data, along with feedback from the field, we made numerous changes that serve to make the ELLCO Pre-K easier to use and score. The most significant changes are the integration of the Literacy Environment Checklist and the Literacy Activities Rating Scale into the architecture of the observation, and the inclusion of detailed descriptive indicators for each of the five scale points. Specific psychometric analyses on the current ELLCO Pre-K will be reported as the tool is used. For reasons that we outline at the end of this appendix, however, we believe that the ELLCO Pre-K will prove to be as reliable, if not more reliable, than the Research Edition.

The ELLCO Toolkit, Research Edition, was pilot tested and used in several research studies from its development, with the minor revisions that typically occur through practical use and feedback, through its original publication in 2002; this included research conducted in more than 150 preschool classrooms for the Head Start–funded New England Quality Research Center (NEQRC) (funder: U.S. Department of Health and Human Services, Administration for Children and Families; 1995–2000) and the Literacy Environment Enrichment Project (LEEP) (funder: U.S. Department of Education, Office of Educational Research and Improvement; 2000–2003), both based in the Center for Children & Families (CC&F) at Education Development Center, Inc., in Newton, Massachusetts. Since its initial publication, researchers at CC&F have used the ELLCO Toolkit, Research Edition, in more than 250 classrooms as part of six different projects:

- The New England Quality Research Center: The Next Generation (funder: U.S. Department of Health and Human Services, Administration for Children and Families; 2001–2006)

- Examining the Efficacy of Two Models of Preschool Professional Development in Language and Literacy (funder: U.S. Department of Education, Institute of Education Sciences; 2005–2007)

- Child Care Quality: Does Partnership Make a Difference—an Extension of the Partnership Impact Project (funder: U.S. Department of Education, 2004–2007)

- Evaluation of the Newport Early Reading First Collaborative (funder: U.S. Department of Education, 2003–2006)

- Evaluation of the Springfield Early Reading First Initiative (funder: U.S. Department of Education, 2003–2007)

- Connecticut Is Reading First (funder: U.S. Department of Education, 2005 to present)

All of these projects are concerned with the language and literacy development of children from lower income families and communities. Because of this, data reported here are based on centers and classrooms in lower income communities.

The data reported in the main body of the appendix come from 30 classrooms from the NEQRC study and a total of 117 classrooms for the LEEP study. Each of the NEQRC classrooms were observed on one occasion, whereas most of the LEEP classrooms were observed on two occasions (fall and spring), and a few LEEP classrooms were visited a total of three times. In the data used to calculate means, correlations, and Cronbach's alpha, each visit to a classroom is counted as a separate observation. In the data used to report stability and change (LEEP classrooms only), each LEEP classroom is counted only once, and fall and spring scores are treated as distinct variables.

An addendum to the original research at the end of this technical appendix describes Cronbach's alpha analyses performed using a larger sample of data collected between 2001 and 2007. These data are from a total of 259 classrooms from the following projects:

- The New England Quality Research Center: The Next Generation ($n = 57$)

- Examining the Efficacy of Two Models of Preschool Professional Development in Language and Literacy ($n = 67$)

- Child Care Quality: Does Partnership Make a Difference—an Extension of the Partnership Impact Project ($n = 66$)

- Evaluation of the Newport Early Reading First Collaborative ($n = 26$)

- Evaluation of the Springfield Early Reading First Initiative ($n = 22$)

- Connecticut Is Reading First ($n = 21$)

As with the data used for the Cronbach's alpha analyses initially reported in the technical appendix of the *User's Guide to the Early Language & Literacy Classroom Observation Toolkit, Research Edition* (Smith & Dickinson, 2002), some classrooms were visited on multiple occasions, and each classroom visit was counted as a separate observation.

PSYCHOMETRIC PROPERTIES OF THE LITERACY ENVIRONMENT CHECKLIST

The psychometric properties presented for the Literacy Environment Checklist (ELLCO Toolkit, Research Edition) are based on data from Year 4 of the NEQRC project combined with data from Years 1–3 of the LEEP project. Data from the NEQRC project were collected during the winter of 1998–1999 ($n = 29$). The data from Year 1 of the LEEP project were collected in the fall of 1998 ($n = 26$) and the spring of 1999 ($n = 26$). Data from Year 2 of the LEEP project were collected in the fall of 1999 ($n = 42$) and spring of 2000 ($n = 38$). Data from Year 3 of the LEEP project were collected in the fall of 2000 ($n = 47$) and spring of 2001 ($n = 47$). Together, the projects resulted in a total sample size of 255, although the actual subsample sizes vary depending on the analyses conducted. Many of the classrooms included were in Head Start programs. Unlike the Classroom Observation, the Literacy Environment Checklist and the Literacy Activities Rating Scale have been used for research only in preschool classrooms and were designed specifically to help identify the impact of our literacy intervention in those classrooms. They have not been used to predict children's growth; rather, they have been used in conjunction with the Classroom Observation to pinpoint the specific effects of a literacy intervention. The items from the Literacy Environment Checklist of the ELLCO Toolkit, Research Edition, have been incorporated into the main body of the ELLCO Pre-K. The Literacy Activities Rating Scale is not included in the ELLCO Pre-K. (See Table A.15 later in this appendix for item-level correspondences between the ELLCO Pre-K and the ELLCO Toolkit, Research Edition.)

Interrater Reliability

Research use of the Literacy Environment Checklist was predicated on the appropriate training of observers. We have required that prospective observers be familiar with theories of early literacy development and have an understanding of the range of instructional methods that are typically used in classrooms.

Prospective observers received a daylong training session on using the ELLCO Toolkit, Research Edition, which included background information on language and literacy development, explanation of the toolkit, and videotape examples; then training session participants received a second day of supervised practice in using the toolkit. When observers were trained and supervised appropriately, we achieved an average interrater reliability of 88% with relative ease. (This interrater reliability rate is for agreements within 1 point of each other on the rating scale.)

General Statistics

On the basis of our theoretical beliefs and preliminary analysis of the data, we created three summary variables for the Literacy Environment Checklist: the *Books* subtotal, the *Writing* subtotal, and the *Total* score. The *Books* subtotal includes all items from the Book Area, Book Selection, and Book Use sections of the checklist. The *Writing* subtotal includes all items from the Writing Materials and Writing Around the Room sections. Table A.1 reports descriptive statistics for Literacy Environment Checklist data gathered as part of the NEQRC and LEEP studies ($n = 255$).

Reliability Analysis

Reliability analysis was conducted to examine the internal consistency of the Literacy Environment Checklist. Table A.2 shows the alphas obtained for the *Total* score as well as for the two subtotals. Cronbach's alpha of .84 for the *Total* score shows good internal consistency. All item–total correlations were moderate to high ($r = .54$ to $r = .55$).

Cronbach's alpha of .73 for the *Books* subtotal shows good internal consistency for this composite. All item–total correlations were moderate ($r = .21$ to $r = .54$) with the exception of Item 1 in the Book Area section ("Is an area set aside just for book reading?"), which exhibited a correlation of .16.

Table A.1.   Descriptive statistics for subscale and total score data for the Literacy Environment Checklist in the ELLCO Toolkit, Research Edition ($n = 255$)

Composite variable	Mean	Standard deviation	Minimum	Maximum
Books subscale	11.13	3.90	2.00	20.00
Writing subscale	10.44	4.22	1.00	20.00
Literacy Environment Checklist Total score	21.57	7.37	5.00	40.00

Table A.2. Cronbach's alpha for data for the Literacy Environment Checklist in the ELLCO Toolkit, Research Edition ($n = 255$)

Composite variable	Alpha
Books subtotal	.73
Writing subtotal	.75
Literacy Environment Checklist Total score	.84

Cronbach's alpha for the *Writing* subtotal was .75, also indicating somewhat low but still acceptable internal consistency. Item–total correlations ranged from a low of .21 for Item 15 in the Writing Materials section ("Are there templates or tools to help children form letters?") to a high of .59 for Item 21 in the Writing Around the Room section ("How many varieties of children's writing are on display in the classroom?").

Measuring Stability and Change

Using the data collected from the LEEP classrooms, we reported preliminary findings on the ability of the Literacy Environment Checklist to measure both stability and change over time (see Table A.3). When one looks at mean scores across the 3 years of the LEEP project, the fall scores of the intervention are

Table A.3. Stability and change in Literacy Environment Checklist scores (ELLCO Toolkit, Research Edition), fall and spring means, for Years 1–3 of the Literacy Environment Enrichment Project (LEEP)

Composite variable	Fall		Spring	
	Comparison group ($n = 38$)	LEEP intervention ($n = 40$)	Comparison group ($n = 38$)	LEEP intervention ($n = 40$)
Books subtotal	9.25	10.53	10.45 ($t = 3.27, p < .01$)	14.84 ($t = 7.18, p < .001$)
Writing subtotal	8.77	11.21	9.12 ($t = 1.14, p = $ n.s.)	14.26 ($t = 5.72, p < .001$)
Literacy Environment Checklist Total score	18.12	20.86	19.52 ($t = 2.87, p < .01$)	29.03 ($t = 7.82, p < .001$)

n.s., not significant.

slightly higher on the three dimensions of the Literacy Environment Checklist than the comparison group. (For the fall scores in the LEEP study, differences between the intervention group and comparison group on the Literacy Environment Checklist were statistically significant for the *Writing* subtotal only ($t = -2.62$, p .05). In the spring, the comparison group showed significant change on the *Total* score as well as on the *Books* subtotal yet remained stable on the *Writing* subtotal. As hoped, the intervention group scores changed significantly from fall to spring in all categories. These changes resulted in intervention group scores that were statistically significantly different from the comparison group scores in every category *and* statistically significantly different from the intervention group fall scores in every category.

PSYCHOMETRIC PROPERTIES OF THE CLASSROOM OBSERVATION

Like the other parts of the ELLCO Toolkit, Research Edition, the Classroom Observation has been used for research for the NEQRC and LEEP. The Classroom Observation also has been used as a part of a school improvement project in the Philadelphia public school system in classrooms that range from kindergarten through grade 5. It has also been introduced to school systems in Connecticut and Maine. In these settings, it is being used both to collect data on and to provide a basis for discussions about classroom quality.

The psychometric properties presented in the sections that follow come from various analyses of data from Year 4 of the NEQRC research project combined with data collected from Years 1–3 of the LEEP project. Data from the NEQRC project were collected during the winter of 1998–1999 ($n = 29$). The data from Year 1 of the LEEP project were collected in the fall of 1998 ($n = 27$) and the spring of 1999 ($n = 27$). Data from Year 2 of the LEEP project were collected in the fall of 1999 ($n = 42$) and spring of 2000 ($n = 38$). Data from Year 3 of the LEEP project were collected in the fall of 2000 and spring of 2001 in New England (fall: $n = 34$; spring: $n = 37$) and North Carolina (fall: $n = 37$; spring: $n = 37$). Together, the projects resulted in a total sample size of 308 classrooms, though the actual subscale size varies depending on the analyses conducted. As with the other parts of the ELLCO Toolkit, the data reported here for the Classroom Observation come from centers and classrooms in lower income communities.

Interrater Reliability

Research use of the Classroom Observation was predicated on appropriate training of observers, as explained in the section of this appendix on the Literacy Environment Checklist. Novice observers' initial observations were conducted with an experienced observer in order to ensure appropriate calibration to the rubrics in the Classroom Observation. When observers were trained and supervised appropriately, we consistently achieved interrater reliabilities of 90% and better for this part of the ELLCO Toolkit.

General Statistics

On the basis of our theoretical beliefs and preliminary analyses of the data, we chose to create three summary variables for the Classroom Observation: the *General Classroom Environment* subtotal, the *Language, Literacy, and Curriculum* subtotal, and the *Total* score. One item (Item 3), Presence and Use of Technology, was problematic[1] and was excluded from all summaries and analyses. Items included in the two subtotals in the ELLCO Toolkit, Research Edition, are as follows.

General Classroom Environment subtotal:

1. Organization of the Classroom
2. Contents of the Classroom
4. Opportunities for Child Choice and Initiative
5. Classroom Management Strategies
6. Classroom Climate

Language, Literacy, and Curriculum subtotal:

7.   Oral Language Facilitation
8.   Presence of Books
9P. Approaches to Book Reading (Prekindergarten and Kindergarten Version)
10P. Approaches to Children's Writing (Prekindergarten and Kindergarten Version)
11. Approaches to Curriculum Integration
12. Recognizing Diversity in the Classroom
13. Facilitating Home Support for Literacy
14. Approaches to Assessment

---

[1] By *problematic*, we mean that scores for Presence and Use of Technology did not cluster with scores for the other items, suggesting that effective use of technology reflects capabilities somewhat distinct from those captured by the other items in the Classroom Observation. In addition the scores for Presence and Use of Technology did not relate clearly to the *General Classroom Environment* subtotal or to the *Language, Literacy, and Curriculum* subtotal; therefore, it was not included in the reported averages or calculations of Cronbach's alpha for the total tool. For this item in 308 classrooms, the mean was 2.45, with a standard deviation of 1.09 and a minimum of 1.0 and a maximum of 5.0.

Table A.4.   Descriptive statistics for data for the Classroom Observation in the ELLCO Toolkit, Research Edition (*n* = 308)

Composite variable	Mean	Standard deviation	Minimum	Maximum
General Classroom Environment subtotal	3.44	0.79	1.20	5.00
Language, Literacy, and Curriculum subtotal	3.02	0.75	1.13	5.00
Classroom Observation Total score	3.15	0.71	1.29	5.00

Using these subtotals, we obtained data from classrooms throughout New England that provide some indication of observed levels of performance in classrooms that serve low-income children. As with the Literacy Environment Checklist, many of the classrooms included were in Head Start programs. Tables A.4 and A.5 report descriptive statistics for the Classroom Observation data gathered as part of the NEQRC and LEEP studies (*n* = 308).

Reliability Analysis

Reliability analysis was conducted to examine the internal consistency of the Classroom Observation using data from 308 classrooms. Table A.6 shows the Cronbach's alphas obtained for the two composites, *General Classroom Environment* and *Language, Literacy, and Curriculum*, and for the *Total* score of all the items on the Classroom Observation that were included in these analyses.

Cronbach's alpha of .83 for the *General Classroom Environment* shows good internal consistency for this composite. All of the item–total correlations

Table A.5.   Frequencies of classrooms (*n* = 308) with Classroom Observation (ELLCO Toolkit, Research Edition) scores in each of the following categories: *high-quality support* (scores ranging from 3.51 to 5), *basic support* (scores ranging from 2.51 to 3.5), and *low-quality support* (scores less than or equal to 2.5)

Composite variable	High-quality support		Basic support		Low-quality support	
General Classroom Environment subtotal	47.4%	(146)	42.2%	(130)	10.4%	(32)
Language, Literacy, and Curriculum subtotal	24.0%	(74)	45.8%	(141)	30.2%	(93)
Classroom Observation Total score	27.9%	(86)	52.6%	(162)	19.5%	(60)

Table A.6. Cronbach's alpha for data for the Classroom Observation in the ELLCO Toolkit, Research Edition ($n = 308$)

Composite variable	Alpha
General Classroom Environment subtotal	.83
Language, Literacy, and Curriculum subtotal	.86
Classroom Observation Total score	.90

were high—with correlation coefficients ranging from .60 for Item 1, Organization of the Classroom, to .75 for Item 6, Classroom Climate—with the exception of Item 2, Contents of the Classroom. This item had the lowest item–total correlation, which was nonetheless a moderate correlation ($r = .53$).

The internal consistency of the *Language, Literacy, and Curriculum* composite is very good, with an alpha of .86. All of the item–total correlations were moderate to high, ranging from .55 for Item 8, Presence of Books, to .65 for Item 13, Facilitating Home Support for Literacy.

Cronbach's alpha of .90 also shows very good internal consistency for all items combined on the Classroom Observation. All of the item–total correlations for the *Classroom Observation Total* were moderate to high ($r = .39$ to $r = .68$).

Measuring Stability and Change

Again, in the LEEP project, classrooms were observed in the fall and in the spring of Years 1–3, yielding the ability to measure change over time using the Classroom Observation. Some of the teachers were taking a yearlong course that focused on early language and literacy (our intervention group); the remaining teachers were not (our comparison group). Using data from the comparison group classrooms, we have data on the ability of the Classroom Observation to measure both stability and change over time (see Table A.7).

The two groups began the fall with similar scores on the three dimensions of the Classroom Observation, with the comparison group scores being slightly lower overall, though not statistically significantly lower, than the intervention group scores. In the spring, the comparison group scores remained stable, though slightly higher overall, with no statistically significant changes from fall to spring. As hoped, the LEEP intervention group scores changed significantly from fall to spring in all categories. These changes resulted in intervention group scores that were statically significantly different from the comparison group scores in every category *and* statistically significantly different from in-

Table A.7. Stability and change in Classroom Observation scores (ELLCO Toolkit, Research Edition), fall and spring means, for Years 1–3 of the Literacy Environment Enrichment Program (LEEP)

	Fall		Spring	
Composite variable	Comparison group ($n = 65$)	LEEP intervention ($n = 42$)	Comparison group ($n = 65$)	LEEP intervention ($n = 42$)
General Classroom Environment subtotal	3.26	3.61	3.42 ($t = 1.96$, $p =$ n.s.)	3.91 ($t = 2.26$, $p < .05$)
Language, Literacy, and Curriculum subtotal	2.85	3.01	2.93 ($t = 1.13$, $p =$ n.s.)	3.75 ($t = 5.50$, $p < .0001$)
Classroom Observation *Total* score	2.97	3.19	3.08 ($t = 1.53$, $p =$ n.s.)	3.74 ($t = 4.88$, $p < .0001$)

n.s., not significant.

tervention group fall scores in every category.

From our comparison group data, we were able to conclude that the Classroom Observation is able to capture *stability* in classroom quality. This is a good indicator of the Classroom Observation's test–retest reliability. Our data also show that the Classroom Observation is able to capture *changes* in classroom quality associated with a literacy-focused intervention. These findings come from two sources: evidence of fall-to-spring growth and differences between the intervention and comparison groups. These data provide evidence of the *instructional sensitivity* of this tool. The concept of instructional sensitivity is an important factor in determining the quality of research instruments. Our data suggest that the Classroom Observation is both stable and sensitive to interventions that target literacy in ways that are consistent with its assumptions about what constitutes appropriate early literacy practices.

Correlation with Another Widely Used Measure

As part of the NEQRC project, the Classroom Observation has been used in conjunction with the Classroom Profile (Abbott-Shim & Sibley, 1998), a widely used tool for assessing the overall quality of early childhood classrooms. One

reason that the Classroom Observation was initially developed was that existing observation tools did not adequately or systematically address early language and literacy experiences or classroom features that are known to support
literacy development (Dickinson & Tabors, 2001). Thus, it was our belief that
the Classroom Observation would exhibit divergent validity when used in conjunction with these other tools, indicating that it is measuring something
qualitatively different. To examine this hypothesis we correlated the *General
Classroom Environment* subtotal, the *Language, Literacy, and Curriculum*
subtotal, and the *Classroom Observation Total* score with the raw scores from
two subscales from the Classroom Profile that we employed, *Learning Environment* and *Scheduling*. We found moderate correlations for all three Classroom Observation variables with scores on the Classroom Profile's *Learning
Environment* subscale ($r = .41, .31$, and $.44$, respectively) but not the profile's
Scheduling subscale ($r = .12, .09$, and $.07$, respectively). We take the finding of
the modest positive relationship to the Classroom Profile's *Learning Environment* subscale as providing convergent validity for the Classroom Observation.
The absence of relationship with the profiles *Scheduling* subscale provides divergent validity because the Classroom Observation was developed to tap a
construct that is distinct from that examined by the *Scheduling* subscale.

Predicting Child Outcomes

Possibly the most important test for a tool that purports to evaluate the quality of support provided for children's literacy development is the capacity of the
tool to predict children's literacy development. The Classroom Observation has
been used in correlational research and employed in hierarchical linear modeling designed to determine the contributions of classroom quality to children's
receptive vocabulary (Peabody Picture Vocabulary Test–Third Edition; Dunn &
Dunn, 1997) and early literacy scores (Profile of Early Literacy Development;
Dickinson & Chaney, 1998). This sophisticated analytic approach allows identification of different sources of variation in children's scores, distinguishing
variation between classrooms that is associated with children's backgrounds
(e.g., income, gender) from variation associated with their classroom experiences. Level 1 models examining between-group variability took into account
variables such as home language (English, Spanish, or other), gender, and age.
The variance in scores that was not accounted for by the background factors
(15% for vocabulary, 20% for literacy) was attributed to classroom factors. Our
models examining sources of classroom-related variance found that scores on
the Classroom Observation accounted for 80% of the between-classroom variance in vocabulary and 67% of the between-classroom variance in early literacy (Dickinson et al., 2000). Although revealing the power of the Classroom
Observation to predict child outcomes, these analyses also provide evidence

that the quality of preschool classrooms attended by children from low-income families can play an important role in supporting their vocabulary growth and early literacy development.

PSYCHOMETRIC PROPERTIES OF
THE LITERACY ACTIVITIES RATING SCALE

Like the Classroom Observation and the Literacy Environment Checklist, the Literacy Activities Rating Scale of the ELLCO Toolkit, Research Edition, has been used to conduct research as part of the NEQRC and LEEP, and the data presented here are from centers and classrooms in lower income communities. The psychometric properties presented for the rating scale are based on data from Year 4 of the NEQRC project, combined with data from Years 1–3 of the LEEP project. Data from the NEQRC project were collected during the winter of 1998–1999 ($n = 30$). The data from Year 1 of the LEEP project were collected in the fall of 1998 ($n = 28$) and the spring of 1999 ($n = 28$). Data from Year 2 of the LEEP project were collected in the fall of 1999 ($n = 42$) and spring of 2000 ($n = 40$). Data from Year 3 of the LEEP project were collected in the fall of 2000 ($n = 47$) and spring of 2001 ($n = 47$). Together, the projects resulted in a total sample size of 262, although actual subsample size varies depending on the analyses conducted. As with the Literacy Environment Checklist, the rating scale has been used for research only in preschool classrooms, many of which are in Head Start programs. Some items from the Literacy Activities Rating Scale have been incorporated into the ELLCO Pre-K (see Table A.15 later in this appendix), but there is no Literacy Activities Rating Scale in the ELLCO Pre-K.

Interrater Reliability

Observers underwent a training process explained in the section of this appendix that describes interrater reliability for the Literacy Environment Checklist and the Classroom Observation. As with those parts of the ELLCO Toolkit, Research Edition, novice observers' initial observations are conducted with an experienced observer. Because the Literacy Activities Rating Scale was used simply to describe activities observed during the classroom visit, we did not maintain formal records of interrater reliability. Observers who visited classrooms together, however, had little difficulty arriving at the same ratings for the classrooms they visited. When observers were trained and supervised appropriately, we achieved an average interrater reliability of 81% with relative ease.

Table A.8. Descriptive statistics for data for the Literacy Activities Rating Scale in the ELLCO Toolkit, Research Edition ($n = 262$)

Composite variable	Mean	Standard deviation	Minimum	Maximum
Full-Group Book Reading subtotal	2.86	1.95	0	6.00
Writing subtotal	2.10	1.39	0	5.00
Literacy Activities Rating Scale *Total* score	5.80	2.63	0	13.00

General Statistics

On the basis of our theoretical beliefs and preliminary analysis of the data, we created three summary variables for the Literacy Activities Rating Scale: the *Full-Group Book Reading* subtotal, the *Writing* subtotal, and the *Total* score. The *Total* score includes all but two items, which were problematic: Item 4 ("Did you observe an adult engaged in one-to-one book reading or small-group book reading?") and Item 5 ("Is time set aside for children to look at books alone or with a friend?"). These two items were excluded from all analyses. The *Full-Group Book Reading* subtotal includes Items 1–3, which address the number of book reading sessions observed, the length of time spent on full-group book reading, and the total number of books read. The *Writing* subtotal includes Items 6–9, which catalog any observations of children writing as well as any instances of adults assisting children with or modeling writing. Table A.8 reports descriptive statistics for Literacy Activities Rating Scale data gathered as part of the NEQRC and LEEP studies ($n = 262$).

Reliability Analysis

Reliability analysis was conducted to examine the internal consistency of the Literacy Activities Rating Scale. Table A.9 shows the alphas obtained for the *Total* score (excluding the two problematic items mentioned previously), as well as the two subtotals. Cronbach's alpha of .66 for the *Total* score shows somewhat low but acceptable internal consistency for this measure. Item–total correlations ranged from a low of .17 for Item 9 ("Did an adult model writing?") to a high of .49 for Item 1 ("How many full-group book-reading sessions did you observe?").

Cronbach's alpha of .92 for the *Full-Group Book Reading* subtotal shows excellent internal consistency for this composite. All item–total correlations were high ($r = .79$ to $r = .88$). The Cronbach's alpha for the *Writing* subtotal was .73, indicating good internal consistency. Item–total correlations were moderate to high, ranging from a low of .37 for Item 9 ("Did an adult model

Table A.9. Cronbach's alpha for data for the Literacy Activities Rating Scale in the ELLCO Toolkit, Research Edition ($n = 262$)

Composite variable	Alpha
Full-Group Book Reading subtotal	.92
Writing subtotal	.73
Literacy Activities Rating Scale Total score	.66

writing?") to a high of .64 for Item 7 ("Did you see children attempting to write letters or words?"). Given the stronger psychometric properties of the two subscales, we advise using the scores on the distinct subscales of the Literacy Activities Rating Scale instead of the total score when analyzing data from this part of the ELLCO Toolkit, Research Edition.

Measuring Stability and Change

Given the data collected from the LEEP classrooms, we have reported preliminary findings on the ability of the Literacy Activities Rating Scale to measure both stability and change over time (see Table A.10). To determine the stabil-

Table A.10. Stability and change in Literacy Activities Rating Scale scores (ELLCO Toolkit, Research Edition), fall and spring means, for Years 1 and 2 of the Literacy Environment Enrichment Project (LEEP)

Composite variable	Fall		Spring	
	Comparison group ($n = 38$)	LEEP intervention ($n = 53$)	Comparison group ($n = 38$)	LEEP intervention ($n = 53$)
Full-Group Book Reading subtotal	2.13	2.79	1.47 ($t = -2.07, p < .05$)	2.89 ($t = 0.28, p =$ n.s.)
Writing subtotal	1.57	2.17	2.16 ($t = 2.81, p < .01$)	2.68 ($t = 2.18, p < .05$)
Literacy Activities Rating Scale score	4.70	5.73	4.70 ($t = 0, p =$ n.s.)	6.68 ($t = 1.94, p =$ n.s.)

n.s., not significant.

ity of the Literacy Activities Rating Scale, we examined the fall and spring scores of the comparison group and LEEP intervention classrooms. We noted that on the *Total* score and the *Full-Group Book Reading* subtotal, the intervention group showed no significant change but that it did show significant change on the *Writing* subtotal. In contrast, the comparison group showed significant changes on both subtotals but not on the total score. We concluded that the Book Reading portion of the Literacy Activities Rating Scale and the overall scale are reasonably stable but that the Writing portion may be relatively more labile, possibly reflecting the developmental changes that occur as children gain literacy skill over the course of the year. Evidence of the *instructional sensitivity* of the Literacy Activities Rating Scale comes from data for the LEEP intervention approach, which we noted reflected significant fall-to-spring change on all dimensions.

CORRELATIONS AMONG THE ELLCO TOOLKIT (RESEARCH EDITION) MEASURES

In Table A.11, we report correlations among the three measures that make up the ELLCO Toolkit, Research Edition ($n = 248$). The variables included in these analyses are as follows:

* The *Books* subtotal, the *Writing* subtotal, the *Literacy Environment Checklist Total*

* The *Language, Literacy, and Curriculum* subtotal; the *General Classroom Environment* subtotal; and the *Classroom Observation Total*

* The *Full-Group Book Reading* subtotal, the *Writing* subtotal, and the *Literacy Activities Rating Scale Total*

We found that the *Language, Literacy, and Curriculum* subtotal and the *General Classroom Environment* subtotal are highly correlated with the *Classroom Observation Total* ($r = .95$ and $.87$ respectively) though not as highly with each other ($r = .69$). This modest correlation between the two subscales of the Classroom Observation provides support for the fact that the two subscales should be examined separately.

In addition, there are moderate-to-strong correlations for all three *Classroom Observation* variables with both the *Books* subtotal ($r = .65, .47,$ and $.62$, respectively) and the *Writing* subtotal ($r = .64, .51,$ and $.63$, respectively) of the Literacy Environment Checklist. The *Literacy Environment Checklist Total* exhibits an even stronger relationship with the *Classroom Observation* scores ($r = .67, .69,$ and $.53$, respectively). The *Books* and *Writing* subtotals for

Table A.11. Correlations for data from New England Quality Research Center (NEQRC) Year 4 and Literacy Environment Enrichment Project (LEEP) Years 1 and 2 ($n = 92$)

Composite variable	Literacy Environment Checklist			Classroom Observation			Literacy Activities Rating Scale	
	1	2	3	4	5	6	7	8
1. Literacy Environment Checklist: Books	—							
2. Literacy Environment Checklist: Writing	.62***	—						
3. Literacy Environment Checklist Total	.89***	.90***	—					
4. Classroom Observation: General Classroom Environment	.47***	.51***	.53***	—				
5. Classroom Observation: Language, Literacy, and Curriculum	.65***	.64***	.69***	.69***	—			
6. Classroom Observation Total	.62***	.63***	.67***	.87***	.95***	—		
7. Literacy Activities Rating Scale: Full-Book Reading	.10	.11	.11	.06	.14*	.11	—	
8. Literacy Activities Rating Scale: Writing	.36***	.43***	.43***	.37***	.47***	.46***	.04	—
9. Literacy Activities Rating Scale Total	.33***	.37***	.38***	.31***	.44***	.41***	.75***	.63***

$*p < .05$ $**p < .01$ $***p < .001$

the checklist are highly correlated with the *Literacy Environment Checklist Total* ($r = .89$ and $.90$, respectively), but not as highly correlated with each other ($r = .62$).

The *Literacy Activities Rating Scale Total* score and the *Writing* subtotal for the rating scale are moderately related to the three *Classroom Observation* scores ($r = .44$, $.31$, and $.41$ respectively, and $r = .47$, $.37$, and $.46$, respectively). Although the *Full-Group Book Reading* subtotal does not show a statistically significant relationship to the *Classroom Observation Total* score ($r = .11$) or the *General Classroom Environment* subtotal ($r = .06$), there is a statistically significant correlation between the *Full-Group Book Reading* subtotal and the *Language, Literacy, and Curriculum* subtotal. The *Literacy Activities Rating Scale Total* score and the *Writing* subtotal are moderately correlated with all three Literacy Environment Checklist scores ($r = .38$, $.33$, and $.37$, respectively, and $r = .43$, $.36$, and $.43$, respectively). The rating scale's *Full-Group Book Reading* and *Writing* subtotals are both highly correlated with the *Literacy Activities Rating Scale Total* score ($r = .75$ and $r = .63$, respectively) yet are not statistically significantly correlated with one another, indicating that the two subscales are measuring different constructs.

ADDENDUM

Cronbach's alpha analyses parallel to those described thus far were performed using a larger sample ($n = 634$) of data collected with the ELLCO Toolkit, Research Edition, between 2002 and 2007. These data come from the following sources:

- The New England Quality Research Center: The Next Generation (2001–2006, $n = 182$)

- Examining the Efficacy of Two Models of Preschool Professional Development in Language and Literacy (2005–2007, $n = 213$)

- Child Care Quality: Does Partnership Make a Difference: An Extension of the Partnership Impact Project (2004–2007, $n = 66$)

- Evaluation of the Newport Early Reading First Collaborative (2003–2006, $n = 66$)

- Evaluation of the Springfield Early Reading First Initiative (2003–2007, $n = 66$)

- Connecticut Is Reading First (2005–2007, $n = 53$)

Table A.12. Cronbach's alpha for larger sample data (2001–2007) for the Literacy Environment Checklist in the ELLCO Toolkit, Research Edition ($n = 616$)

Composite variable	Alpha
Books subtotal	.76
Writing subtotal	.75
Literacy Environment Checklist Total score	.84

Results of the Cronbach's alpha analyses, described in detail next for each section of the ELLCO Toolkit, Research Edition, corroborate the other findings reported in this appendix and thereby strengthen confidence in the internal reliability of the tool.

Alpha coefficients for the *Literacy Environment Checklist Total* score as well as the *Books* and *Writing* subtotals all show good internal consistency (see Table A.12). Item–total correlations for the *Books* subtotal were moderate, ranging from .23 to .59. Item–total correlations for the *Writing* subtotal also were moderate ($r = .23$ to $r = .53$), with the exception of Item 13 ("Is an alphabet visible?") and Item 24 ("Are there puzzles with words available for children's use?") ($r = .17$ for both). Those two items also exhibited low item–total correlation with the *Literacy Environment Checklist Total* score ($r = .13$ and .16, respectively), whereas the remaining items displayed moderate ($r = .21$ to $r = .57$) item–total correlation with the total score.

The Cronbach's alpha coefficients for the *General Classroom Environment* subtotal, the *Language, Literacy, and Curriculum* subtotal and the *Classroom Observation Total* score all show good to excellent internal consistency (Table A.13). Furthermore, both of the Classroom Observation subtotals as well as the *Total* score exhibited moderate to high item–total correlations, ranging from .57 to .73 for the *General Classroom Environment* subscale, .60 to .73 for the *Language, Literacy, and Curriculum* subscale, and .56 to .77 for the *Total* score.

Table A.13. Cronbach's alpha for larger sample data (2001–2007) for the Classroom Observation in the ELLCO Toolkit, Research Edition ($n = 634$)

Composite variable	Alpha
General Classroom Environment subtotal	.84
Language, Literacy, and Curriculum subtotal	.89
Classroom Observation Total score	.93

Table A.14. Cronbach's alpha for larger sample data (2001–2007) for the Literacy Activities Rating Scale in the ELLCO Toolkit, Research Edition ($n = 547$)

Composite variable	Alpha
Full-Group Book Reading subtotal	.90
Writing subtotal	.74
Literacy Activities Rating Scale total score	.72

In Table A.14, the *Full-Group Book Reading* alpha of .90 shows very good internal consistency for this subtotal. The *Writing* subtotal and *Literacy Activity Rating Scale Total* score both show good internal consistency with alphas of .74 and .72, respectively. Item–total correlations for the *Full-Group Book Reading* subscale were high, ranging from .75 to .85. The items that compose the *Writing* subtotal showed moderate to high item–total correlations of .47 to .64. The *Literacy Activities Rating Scale Total* score also had moderate to high item–total correlations that ranged from .30 to .56.

On the basis of on the psychometric properties of the ELLCO Toolkit, Research Edition, as well as the theoretical and practical considerations outlined in Chapter 1, we revised the ELLCO to include more specificity, in the form of detailed descriptive indicators for each scale point, as well as a broader range of measures of quality in early literacy, such as phonological awareness, efforts to build vocabulary, opportunities for extended conversations, and environmental print. Although the ELLCO Pre-K is more thorough and expansive than the Research Edition, it does include the same content covered by the earlier version, with the exception of Research Edition Item 3: Presence and Use of Technology. Cronbach's alpha analyses on the ELLCO Toolkit, Research Edition, described earlier in this technical appendix, indicated that this construct was not statistically related to the other items; therefore, it was not included in the ELLCO Pre-K.

Users of the ELLCO Pre-K who are familiar with the Research Edition will notice that there is now less emphasis on teacher responses to the Teacher Interview, which, in the Research Edition, informed scoring decisions for several items (e.g., Item 13: Facilitation of Home Support for Literacy, Item 14: Approaches to Assessment). Aspects of these and other items from the Research Edition have now been integrated with items in the Pre-K version. All items are now based predominantly on observable classroom indicators to increase validity and reliability. Table A.15 outlines the relationship between the items in the ELLCO Pre-K and the ELLCO Toolkit, Research Edition.

Given that the ELLCO Pre-K includes the content covered in the Research Edition while providing more specificity and a broader range of items, we have every reason to believe that the ELLCO Pre-K will exhibit similar, if not

Table A.15. Item–level correspondences between ELLCO Pre-K and ELLCO Toolkit, Research Edition

ELLCO Pre-K item	Related items from ELLCO Toolkit, Research Edition
1. Organization of the Classroom	Classroom Observation 1. Organization of the Classroom
2. Contents of the Classroom	Classroom Observation 2. Contents of the Classroom
3. Classroom Management	Classroom Observation 5. Classroom Management Strategies
4. Personnel	N/A (item new to ELLCO Pre-K)
5. Approaches to Curriculum	Classroom Observation 11. Approaches to Curriculum Integration
6. Opportunities for Child Choice and Initiative	Classroom Observation 4. Opportunities for Child Choice and Initiative
7. Recognizing Diversity in the Classroom	Classroom Observation 12. Recognizing Diversity in the Classroom Aspects of Classroom Observation 13. Facilitating Home Support for Literacy
8. Discourse Climate	Aspects of Classroom Observation 6. Classroom Climate
9. Opportunities for Extended Conversations	Aspects of Classroom Observation 7. Oral Language Facilitation Aspects of Classroom Observation 14. Approaches to Assessment
10. Efforts to Build Vocabulary	Aspects of Classroom Observation 7. Oral Language Facilitation
11. Phonological Awareness	N/A (item new to ELLCO Pre-K)
12. Organization of Book Area	Aspects of Classroom Observation 8. Presence of Books Literacy Environment Checklist Items 1, 2
13. Characteristics of Books	Aspects of Classroom Observation 8. Presence of Books Literacy Environment Checklist Items 4, 6
14. Books for Learning	N/A (item new to ELLCO Pre-K)
15. Approaches to Book Reading	Aspects of Classroom Observation 9P. Approaches to Book Reading Literacy Activities Rating Scale Items 1, 4, 5
16. Quality of Book Reading	Aspects of Classroom Observation 9P. Approaches to Book Reading
17. Early Writing Environment	Aspects of Classroom Observation 10P. Approaches to Children's Writing Literacy Environment Checklist Items 13, 14, 15, 18, 19, 20, 22a, 22b
18. Support for Children's Writing	Aspect of Classroom Observation 10P. Approaches to Children's Writing Literacy Activities Rating Scale Items 6, 7, 8, 9
19. Environmental Print	N/A (item new to ELLCO Pre-K)

stronger, psychometric properties than the Research Edition. Because both instruments share the same general structure, it is appropriate to compare the ELLCO Pre-K and the Classroom Observation from the Research Edition. The ELLCO Pre-K includes 19 items, whereas the Classroom Observation contains 14 items. If all else remains constant, the mere increase in the number of items allows for more variance, which should lead to increased reliability of the overall scale. Given the greater level of detail provided by having descriptive indicators for each scale point, we would also anticipate improved levels of interrater reliability. Clearly, this hypothesis will need to be verified empirically; therefore, we are currently collecting data on the ELLCO Pre-K in order to perform psychometric analyses, the findings of which will be provided online at http://www.brookespublishing.com/ellco in the near future.

REFERENCES

Abbott-Shim, M., & Sibley, A. (1998). *Assessment Profile for Early Childhood Programs.* Atlanta, GA: Quality Assist.

Dickinson, D.K., & Chaney, C. (1998). *Profile of Early Literacy Development.* Newton, MA: Education Development Center, Inc.

Dickinson, D.K., Sprague, K., Sayer, A., Miller, C., Clark, N., & Wolf, A. (2000). Classroom factors that foster literacy and social development of children from different language backgrounds. In M. Hopman (Chair), *Dimensions of program quality that foster child development: Reports from 5 years of the Head Start Quality Research Centers.* Poster session presented at the biannual National Head Start Research Conference, Washington, DC.

Dickinson, D.K., & Tabors, P.O. (Eds.). (2001). *Beginning literacy with language: Young children learning at home and school.* Baltimore: Paul H. Brookes Publishing Co.

Dunn, L.M., & Dunn, L.M. (1997). *Peabody Picture Vocabulary Test–Third Edition.* Circle Pines, MN: American Guidance Service.

Smith, M.W., & Dickinson, D.K. (with Sangeorge, A., & Anastasopoulos, L.). (2002). *User's Guide to the Early Language & Literacy Classroom Observation Toolkit* (Research ed.). Baltimore: Paul H. Brookes Publishing Co.

Resources

WEB SITES

American Library Association Book Lists

http://www.ala.org/ala/alsc/alscresources/booklists/booklists.htm

The American Library Association seeks to promote high-quality library and information services. This web site provides parents, teachers, and child care providers with booklists for children, with different lists based around ages, cultural backgrounds, and themes. Two lists of particular relevance are

ALA Bilingual Books for Children

http://www.ala.org/ala/alsc/alscresources/booklists/bilingual books.htm

This list compiles books for children from birth to age 14. Each book has bilingual text, and the list is organized by language. Books with text in 12 different languages are included, with an extensive section on books with Spanish text.

ALA Suggested Books

http://www.ala.org/ala/alsc/alscresources/booklists/suggested books.htm

This region provides a book list that was compiled by a Reading Is Fundamental committee. The list is organized by age group and provides titles and author information on recommended books for children birth to age 14.

Aspectos Culturales

http://www.aspectosculturales.com

This web site aims to improve cultural awareness in children and adults and improve the understanding and use of the Spanish language by teachers, children, and other adults. It provides teachers and other adults with resources and ideas for raising their awareness of Hispanic language and culture, as well as strategies for how to incorporate this awareness into the classroom. Ideas for books, games, music, resources, and activities geared at building awareness and integration are included.

Improving Access and Opportunity for Latinos in Early Childhood—Resources

http://ccf.edc.org/latinos/id3.htm

This list presents a selection of resources in both English and Spanish to support the cultural and linguistic responsiveness of early childhood programs.

International Reading Association

http://www.reading.org

The International Reading Association (IRA) is a professional organization for individuals involved in teaching reading. The organization's web site provides membership information; links to key publications of the IRA; a list of useful web resources including lesson plans, booklists, and parent resources; an on-line store; and links to other relevant and important web sites for reading teachers.

Literacy Coaching Clearinghouse

http://www.literacycoachingonline.org

The Literacy Coaching Clearinghouse is a joint venture of the International Reading Association and the National Council of Teachers of English. Its mission is to "increase the knowledge base, research, and practice of literacy coaching." This web site provides an overview of literacy coaching, a set of brief publications, a more extensive list of collected key resources, a section on literacy coaching programs, links to key organizations in literacy coaching, a literacy coaching blog, and postings about events that might be of interest to practitioners.

National Association for the Education of Young Children (NAEYC)

http://www.naeyc.org

NAEYC is the world's largest organization working in the interest of children birth through age 8. Its focus is on ensuring that all young children receive quality educational and developmental services; it has a network of several hundred state and local affiliates dedicated to pursuing its mission. NAEYC's web site provides important information on accreditation, conferences, membership, public policy, and early childhood.

National Center for Family Literacy
http://www.famlit.org

The National Center for Family Literacy seeks to use the power inherent in families to help solve the literacy crisis. The center creates and funds initiatives across the United States, some of which target children from diverse backgrounds, which support family literacy, and which promote the joint role of parents and teachers in fostering literacy in children. The web site describes the center's mission and methods and provides information for parents and teachers on how they can benefit from the center's work.

National Institute for Literacy
http://nifl.gov

The National Institute for Literacy is a federal agency that provides leadership and information on literacy issues. The institute is especially focused on improving language and literacy instruction for children and adults. The web site provides information and downloadable guides on language and literacy development and instruction for both teachers and parents.

PBS Parents Web Site
http://www.pbs.org/parents

The PBS Parents web site is hosted by PBS and provides games, activities, and parenting advice for parents of children of all ages. The web site provides parent and child care providers with guides on child development, children and media, creativity, early math, going to school, raising boys, reading and language, and talking with children. Three regions of the web site are particularly relevant:

Bookfinder
http://www.pbs.org/parents/bookfinder

The PBS Parents Bookfinder region provides parents and child care providers with a search engine for age-appropriate, high-quality children's books. The search can be conducted by age, book theme, or specific search terms and includes a list of high-quality books with author information and book descriptions. The search also includes Spanish-language books.

Creativity

http://www.pbs.org/parents/creativity

The PBS Parents Creativity region is a set of online tools and activities designed to help parents explore creativity with their children. Activities include simple games and ideas for off-line activities that foster children's intellectual engagement.

Reading/Language

http://www.pbs.org/parents/readinglanguage

The PBS Parents Reading/Language region provides parents with research-based information on reading and language development from birth to third grade. It presents milestones for each age, as well as key strategies for helping children of that age with appropriate language and learning support as they develop their emergent literacy skills.

Reading Is Fundamental—Leamos en familia!

http://www.rif.org/leer

This Spanish version of the Reading Is Fundamental web site provides ideas and activities for families to explore reading in their everyday lives. The web site is organized around different rooms in a house, which function as themes around which activities are structured.

Reading Rockets

http://www.readingrockets.org

Reading Rockets is a multimedia project that provides information on how children learn to read and resources to help parents and educators support literacy development. The web site has pages that offer techniques for teaching children to read, strategies for helping struggling readers, and a search tool for recommended books for young children. In addition, the web site houses multimedia resources, including videos, webcasts, and podcasts about early literacy development, as well as links to other resources. The web site is also accessible in Spanish.

Scientific Council on the Developing Child

http://www.developingchild.net

The Scientific Council on the Developing Child is a multidisciplinary organization whose mission is to bridge the gap between the science of early child development and public decision making and policy. The web site provides an overview of the council's work as well as downloadable documents and links to key council publications.

WEB RESOURCES

A Child Becomes a Reader: Birth through Preschool

http://www.nifl.gov/partnershipforreading/publications/pdf/ low_res_child_reader_B-K.pdf

This comprehensive guide for parents of children birth to kindergarten includes a summary of research findings on the building blocks of reading and writing. It outlines activities that parents can do with their children to help foster emergent literacy skills, as well as literacy milestones that children should reach between birth and age 4. The guide also suggests to parents what they should look for in child care and preschool centers with regard to early literacy. Finally, it includes a list of helpful terms and a bibliography of suggested readings and resources for parents and caregivers.

Literacy Development in the Preschool Years

http://www.reading.org/downloads/positions/ps1066_preschool.pdf

This 2005 position statement outlines the International Reading Association's views on effective practices in literacy instruction for preschoolers. The document outlines the evidence behind effective strategies and gives key recommendations for preschool educators, parents, and policymakers.

Parent Involvement in Early Literacy

Lin, Q. (2003). *Parent involvement and early literacy* (Research Digest). Cambridge, MA: Harvard Family Research Project.

http://www.gse.harvard.edu/hfrp/projects/fine/resources/digest/literacy.html

This document summarizes a research study on parent involvement in early literacy. The authors argue for the importance of home–school connections in fostering emergent literacy and make several key recommendations for how school personnel can enhance these connections.

Put Reading First: Helping Your Child Learn to Read.
Parent Guide: Preschool Through Grade 3

http://www.nifl.gov/partnershipforreading/publications/Parent_br.pdf

This parent guide gives a short overview of the National Reading Panel findings and provides suggestions for what to expect from a school reading program based on scientific research. The guide ends with a section on how parents can reinforce their children's early literacy development with activities and games in the home.

Quality of Childcare Affects Language Development

FPG Child Development Institute. (2007). Quality of childcare affects language development [Electronic version]. *FPG Snapshot,* (No. 40, February), 1–2.

http://www.fpg.unc.edu/~snapshots/snap40.pdf

This research snapshot argues that children in high-quality child care settings experience greater language development, especially when measured in terms of vocabulary development. The authors suggest that this might be because of the level of interaction between child care staff and children in higher quality settings, and they present evidence that these differences are amplified over time spent in different settings.

What Is Scientifically Based Research? A Guide for Teachers

http://www.nifl.gov/partnershipforreading/publications/science_research.pdf

This teacher-oriented guide provides a quick overview of what scientifically based research is and why it is important in instructional design. It provides a basic summary of how scientific evaluation research works and suggestions for how research can be translated into classroom practice.

RESEARCH ARTICLES, BOOKS, AND BOOK CHAPTERS

Biemiller, A. (2006). Vocabulary development and instruction: A prerequisite for school learning. In D.K. Dickinson & S.B. Neuman (Eds.), *Handbook of early literacy research* (Vol. 2, pp. 41–51). New York: Guilford Press.

This chapter discusses the important links between early vocabulary and later literacy. It discusses the scientific evidence for this link, emphasizing the size and sequence of vocabulary development and the importance of acquiring word meaning. Finally, it discusses practical implications of this research for teachers in classroom settings.

Bowman, B. (Ed.). (2002). *Love to read: Essays in developing and enhancing early literacy skills of African American children.* Washington, DC: National Black Child Development Institute.

This collection of essays arises out of a growing concern about the disparity in literacy and school performance between African American and Caucasian children. These essays, collected from leading scholars in early literacy education, address pertinent issues ranging from the social and economic causes for this performance gap, to scientific evidence for best literacy practices, to suggestions for how best to help enhance African American children's early literacy skills at an early age.

Dickinson, D.K., & Brady, J.P. (2005). Toward effective support for language and literacy through professional development. In M. Zaslow & I. Martinez-Beck (Eds.), *Critical issues in early childhood professional development* (pp. 141–170). Baltimore: Paul H. Brookes Publishing Co.

This chapter describes the need for professional development programs that enhance teacher's early language and literacy support to children from low-income backgrounds. The authors report on the development of several models of professional development, their success, and lessons learned.

Dickinson, D.K., McCabe, A., Anastasopoulos, L., Peisner-Feinberg, E.S., & Poe, M.D. (2003). The comprehensive language approach to early literacy: The interrelationships among vocabulary, phonological sensitivity, and print knowledge among preschool-aged children. *Journal of Educational Psychology, 95*(3), 465–481.

This research article presents a novel framework for understanding the interrelatedness of vocabulary, oral language, and print understanding in preschool children. The authors argue that prior research has discounted the interactions between these domains and thus has underestimated the importance of oral language skills in learning to read.

Dickinson, D.K., McCabe, A., & Clark-Chiarelli, N. (2004). Preschool-based prevention of reading disability: Realities vs. possibilities. In A. Stone, E. Silliman, B.J. Ehren, & K. Apel (Eds.), *Handbook of language and literacy: Development and disorders* (pp. 209–227). Mahwah, NJ: Lawrence Erlbaum Associates.

This chapter discusses the issue of using the preschool classroom as a setting to help reduce the incidence of learning disabilities. The authors review evidence from scientific research on the incidence and prevention of learning disabilities in young children and discuss both the potential and limitations for early childhood classrooms as a prevention setting.

Dickinson, D.K., McCabe, A., & Essex, M.J. (2006). A window of opportunity we must open to all: The case for preschool with high-quality support for language and literacy. In D.K. Dickinson & S.B. Neuman (Eds.), *Handbook of early literacy research* (Vol. 2, pp. 11–28). New York: Guilford Press.

This chapter presents scientific evidence from research in early literacy, social and emotional development, and brain development, making the case for early language and literacy support in preschool classrooms. The authors argue that evidence clearly demonstrates the interdependencies between these three domains of development and that effective instruction between ages 3 and 5 is especially important for long-term development.

Dickinson, D.K., & Neuman, S.B. (Eds.). (2006). *Handbook of early literacy research* (Vol. 2). New York: Guilford Press.

This volume presents a wealth of information on the findings of scientific early literacy research. It is broken down into several broad areas of research and highlights key findings that are vital to understanding children's early literacy development and implications for literacy support and instruction. (See individual chapter descriptions for more detailed annotation.)

Eggers-Piérola, C. (2005). *Connections and commitments: Reflecting Latino values in early childhood programs.* Portsmouth, NH: Heinemann.

This book provides a framework for early childhood educators to help them teach Latino students more effectively and work to incorporate them fully into the early childhood classroom. The book emphasizes four key values that are critical to making connections with Latino children and their families and devotes several sections to language, literacy, and bilingualism.

Farran, D.C., Aydogan, C., Kang, S.J., & Lipsey, M.W. (2006). Preschool classroom environments and the quantity and quality of children's literacy and language behaviors. In D.K. Dickinson & S.B. Neuman (Eds.), *Handbook of early literacy research* (Vol. 2, pp. 257–268). New York: Guilford Press.

This chapter stresses the importance of classroom environments in children's early literacy development and makes the argument that classrooms can be used for language and literacy interventions for children from low-income families. It reviews different practices that might be effective and discusses the difficulties encountered when identifying the most promising language facilitating activities.

Gillespie, J.T. (2002). *Best books for children—preschool through grade 6* (7th ed.). Westport, CT: Libraries Unlimited.

This book is an encyclopedic list of books for children of all ages, organized by type of book (e.g., space exploration, picture books). It provides age recommendations, publisher information, and one-sentence descriptions of each of the more than 20,000 books it lists.

Hirschler, J.A. (2005). How teachers support English language learners in the classroom. *Head Start Bulletin* (78), 31–32.

This article provides illustrative examples of strategies that various teachers use in supporting English-language learners in the classroom. It provides teachers with a few key points about what strategies seem most effective and what issues they should be aware of.

Korat, O., Bahar, E., & Snapir, M. (2003). Sociodramatic play as opportunity for literacy development: The teacher's role. *The Reading Teacher, 56*(4), 386–393.

This article discusses a project in one teacher's classroom in which the teacher used sociodramatic play to facilitate learning of written language. The authors argue that this example illustrates that children actively use their prior assumptions about how written language works in their play.

Lonigan, C.J. (2003). Development and promotion of emergent literacy skills in children at-risk of reading difficulties. In B.R. Foorman (Ed.), *Preventing and remediating reading difficulties: Bringing science to scale* (pp. 23–50). Timonium, MD: York Press.

This chapter discusses the importance of promoting emergent literacy skills in young children—in particular the domains of oral language, print knowledge, and phonological awareness. The author argues that providing a solid foundation in the precursors to full literacy is vital, especially to children who are at high risk of developing reading difficulties, as failing to grasp these early building blocks will greatly reduce the likelihood that they will achieve full literacy.

Opitz, M.F. (2000). *Rhymes and reasons: Literature and language play for phonological awareness*. Portsmouth, NH: Heinemann.

This book provides an alternative to phonics-based reading instruction, based on various types of language play that facilitate phonological awareness. It provides a detailed guide to various aspects of phonological awareness and ideas for types of activities, games, and free-play that promote it. Finally, the book includes a list of more than 350 books featuring language play and other activities that can be read aloud to facilitate language development.

Schickedanz, J.A., & Casbergue, R.M. (2004). *Writing in preschool: Learning to orchestrate meaning and marks*. Newark, DE: International Reading Association.

This book focuses on preschoolers' writing development, from early scribbles to coherent, meaningful sentences. The authors provide exhaustive insight into how environments and teachers can best facilitate children's early learning of writing systems and how teachers can foster excitement and enthusiasm about the world of written words.

Strickland, D.S., & Shanahan, T. (2004). Laying the groundwork for literacy. *Educational Leadership, 61*(6), 74–77.

This article reviews the findings of the National Early Literacy Panel. Specifically, the authors argue that the findings of the panel suggest that early development in the broad areas of oral language, alphabetic knowledge, and print knowledge are vital to children's later literacy.